LINDLEY

&

BANKS

ON

PARTNERSHIP

FIRST SUPPLEMENT
TO THE
EIGHTEENTH EDITION

BY

R. C. I'ANSON BANKS, LL.B.
of Lincoln's Inn, Barrister

LONDON
Sweet & Maxwell
2005

"A Treatise on the Law of Partnership, including its application to Companies,"
  first edition (in two volumes) by Nathaniel Lindley, afters Lord Lindley,
  M.R., and a Lord of Appeal   1860
Second Edition by the Author   1867
Third Edition by the Author   1873
Fourth Edition by the Author   1878
The work was divided in *Lindley on Companies* (one volume) and *Lindley on
  Partnership* (one volume), each by the Author in   1888
Sixth Edition by the Hon. W. B. Lindley   1893
Seventh Edition by Judge the Hon. W. B. Lindley and T. J. C. Tomlin   1905
Eighth Edition by Judge the Hon. W. B. Lindley and A. Andrews Uthwatt   1912
Ninth Edition by Judge the Hon. W. B. Lindley   1924
Tenth Edition by Judge the Hon. W. B. Lindley   1935
Eleventh Edition by Henry Salt, K.C., and Hugh E. Frances   1950
Twelfth Edition by Ernest H. Scamell   1962
Thirteenth Edition by Ernest H. Scamell   1971
Fourteenth Edition by Ernest H. Scamell and R. C. I'Anson Banks   1979
Fifteenth Edition by Ernest H. Scamell and R. C. I'Anson Banks   1984
Sixteenth Edition by R. C. I'Anson Banks   1990
Seventeenth Edition by R. C. I'Anson Banks   1995
Eighteenth Edition by R. C. I'Anson Banks   2002
  First Supplement by R. C. I'Anson Banks   2005

Published in 2005 by
Sweet & Maxwell Limited of
100 Avenue Road London NW3 3PF
(http://www.sweetandmaxwell.co.uk)

Computerset by Interactive Sciences Ltd, Gloucester
Printed in England by Athenaeum Press Ltd, Gateshead

ISBN 0421 915005

A catalogue record for this book is available from the British Library

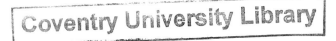

LINDLEY

&

BANKS

ON

PARTNERSHIP

AUSTRALIA
Law Book Co.
Sydney

CANADA and USA
Carswell
Toronto

HONG KONG
Sweet & Maxwell
Asia

NEW ZEALAND
Brookers
Wellington

SINGAPORE and MALAYSIA
Sweet & Maxwell Asia
Singapore and Kuala Lumpur

HOW TO USE THIS SUPPLEMENT

This is the First Supplement to the Eighteenth Edition of *Lindley & Banks on Partnership*, and has been compiled according to the structure of the main volume.

At the beginning of each chapter of this Supplement is a mini table of contents from the main volume updated as required to reflect the contents of this Supplement. Where a heading in this table of contents has been marked with a square pointer, this indicates that there is relevant information in the Supplement to which the reader should refer. Material that updates a section in the Eighteenth Edition is indicated by the symbol ■.

Within each chapter, updating information is referenced to the relevant paragraph in the main volume, save where new paragraphs have been added.

PREFACE

As far as I am aware this is the first ever supplement to this work, to be published only three years after the 18th edition. This is a measure not only of the increasing profile of partnership and partnership related topics, but also of ever changing legislation and the continuing proliferation of decided cases. As I write this, we appear to be facing another period of upheaval. It is clear that the limited liability partnership has now gained ready acceptance both within and outside the professions, but the attitude of the courts to this vehicle remains something of an open question. Whether partnership law will be applied by analogy, particularly in those cases where the duty of good faith has been imported into the LLP environment, is unclear, although I detect a slightly alarming tendency in such decided cases as there have been to treat them as "just another form of partnership". It would seem that true partnership law cannot be written off just yet. Although the Government appears to have little appetite for enacting the root and branch changes recommended by the Law Commission in its 2003 Report on Partnership Law, even the much needed update of limited partnership law currently appears to have been sidelined. This is regrettable, particularly as it has been announced that the most radical of the Clementi proposals (as well as provisions permitting the creation of MDPs) are likely to be enacted before the end of 2006. These reforms, although initially confined to the legal profession, are, ultimately, likely to impact in other areas.

Coupled with these changes, the downgrading of the expressions "partner" and "partnership", which I have noted in previous editions, continues unabated: soon section 2 of the Partnership Act 1890 will establish when a "civil partner" of a partner is not to be regarded as a partner! Need I say more?

There have, of course, been numerous decided cases of importance since the 18th edition was published. Most notable, in terms of third party claims, is the House of Lords' decision in *Dubai Aluminium Co Ltd v. Salaam*, which, predictably, re-establishes something approaching a presumption of liability in partnership cases, despite the temporary blip caused by the Court of Appeal, as noted in the preface to that edition. The appeal in *Walker v. Stones*, *Dubai Aluminium's* travelling companion, was in the event never heard. The impact which *Dubai Aluminium* has had is amply illustrated in *J.J. Coughlan v. Ruparelia* and this trend may well, ultimately, spill over into the limited liability partnership field where the personal liability of members remains a hot topic. Lord Millett's *obiter* views on repudiation in *Hurst v. Bryk* have, as expected, been adopted and applied by Neuberger J. in *Mullins v. Laughton*, even if some of the reasoning in that case is open to question, as discussed *infra*, paras 24–05 *et seq*. Repudiation can now, in large measure, be regarded as a dead letter in partnership law terms. There have, of course, been other interesting cases, particularly the Court of Appeal's decision in *Chahal v. Mahal*, regarding the effects of incorporation on the continuing existence of a firm, but not all have been properly reported, which is a matter of regret.

On the statutory front, further wide-ranging anti-discrimination laws have been imposed on partnerships, still without sufficient account being taken of the unique nature of this business vehicle, as exemplified by the now well-established practice of tucking the necessary statutory provisions away in what are styled "Employment Equality Regulations". That internal partnership issues should be decided in the Employment Tribunal is a measure of this "one size fits all" approach and the long term implications become clearer as the number of discrimination claims steadily increases. The deficiencies of the whole legislative approach are thrown into sharp relief by the decision of the Employment Appeal Tribunal in *Dave v. Robinska*. The problem will be further compounded by the introduction of the proposed age discrimination legislation in 2006, which seem likely further to undermine established and traditional partnership practices, such as the profit sharing lockstep. Attempts to seek exemption for such practices seem doomed to fail.

On the tax front, the Income Tax (Trading and Other Income) Act 2005 has supplanted many (but, typically, not all) of the applicable provisions of the Income and Corporation Taxes Act 1988, merely creating a *different* patchwork of legislation for the practitioner to toil through. However, this pales into insignificance when compared with the new stamp duty land tax legislation applicable to partnership transactions, as introduced by the Finance Act 2004. In an understandable attempt to counter abuses of the old stamp duty regime, these provisions, though relatively short, are of labyrinthine complexity and show little apparent understanding of how partnerships actually operate. We now appear to have the concept of "deemed" partnership property introduced through a side door. I have done what I can to steer the reader towards an understanding of how the legislation *appears* to work. More welcome is, perhaps, HM Revenue & Customs' clarification of the value added tax treatment of the assignment of a partnership share, a subject which I endeavoured to analyse in previous editions with no official guidance whatsoever.

As always, my thanks are due to the staff at Sweet & Maxwell for their patience when deadlines slipped and for making sure that this supplement was produced before 2005 drew to a close. On a more personal note, I am well aware that my wife, Susie, had to bear the brunt of the pressures caused by this supplement alone, since my sons are now both off at university and completely insulated from the writing process. To her I unhesitatingly extend my heartfelt gratitude and love.

The law is, so far as possible, stated as at September 15, 2005 although prospective changes are, where relevant, noted.

Roderick I'Anson Banks   October 19, 2005
48 Bedford Row
London WC1

TABLE OF CASES

TABLE OF STATUTES

TABLE OF STATUTORY INSTRUMENTS

Part One

THE NATURE OF PARTNERSHIP

CHAPTER 1

INTRODUCTION

1. ORIGIN OF THE LAW OF PARTNERSHIP

Limited liability partnerships

NOTE 5. This footnote should refer to the Limited Liability Partnerships Regula-   **1–03**
tions 2001, reg.7, rather than *ibid.* reg.6.

DEFINITION OF PARTNERSHIP

1. DEFINITION IN THE PARTNERSHIP ACT 1890

2–01 The same conditions must be satisfied when a new partner joins an existing firm pursuant to an assignment of another partner's share: see para.19–68. The continued satisfaction of those conditions cannot simply be assumed because there is an existing firm: see *Backman v. R*, 3 I.T.L. Rep. 647, at [40]–[42] (Sup Ct (Can)).

A. THE BUSINESS

2–02 It naturally does not matter whether the business is a new business or an existing business, nor for how long it is carried on: *Backman v. R, supra*, at [20].

Interruption to business

2–04 It now seems clear that the sale of the *entire* partnership business to a company owned by the firm will not *per se* prevent a partnership continuing to exist, particularly if the partnership business can be regarded as extending to the business carried on through the medium of the company or other special circumstances exist: *Chahal v. Mahal*, September 30, 2004 (Lawtel 5/10/04), at [90]–[94], affirmed at [2005] EWCA Civ 898 (Lawtel 18/7/05).

B. TWO OR MORE PERSONS CARRYING ON A BUSINESS IN COMMON

2–05 Equally, if the business is disposed of almost as soon as the "partnership" is formed, this may not satisfy the requirement: *Backman v. R*, 3 I.T.L. Rep. 647, at [28] (Sup Ct (Can)).

Note 14. See also *Chahal v. Mahal*, September 30, 2004 (Lawtel 5/1/04), at [80].

A business carried on "in common"

Note 19. See also *Backman v. R, supra*, at [21].   **2–06**

C. "With a View of Profit"

The *amount* of the profit to be realised by the venture does not matter, unless it   **2–07**
is, on a true analysis, *de minimis*: *Backman v. R*, 3 I.T.L. Rep. 647, (Sup Ct
(Can)).

Note 27. See also *Backman v. R, supra*.

Note 29. See also *Backman v. R, supra*.   **2–08**

E. The Normal Incidents of Partnership

Partnership a contractual relationship

Note 59. For a recent affirmation of this, see *Philips v. Symes* [2002] 1 W.L.R.   **2–13**
853, at [43], *per* Hart J.

2. Contemplated Partnerships

Business not yet commenced

Note 63. Note, however the approach adopted by Lord Macfadyen in *Small v.*   **2–15**
Fleming, 2003 S.C.L.R. 647, OH, when considering whether a joint venture
(which he described as a "species of partnership") existed between the
parties.

(b) Application of the Principle: Promoters of Companies

Note 82. See also *Ness Training Ltd v. Triage Central Ltd*, 2002 S.L.T. 675,   **2–26**
OH.

3. Associations not Governed by the Partnership Act 1890

Limited liability partnerships

Note 18. The *Williams v. Natural Life Health Foods Ltd* approach found favour   **2–37**
in *Bradford & Bingley Plc v. Martin Hayes, Dunphy & Hayes Ltd*, 2001 WL

1560784, whereas *Merrett v. Babb* appears to have been favoured by the court in *Yazhou Travel Investment Company Ltd v. Bateman Starr* [2005] P.N.L.R. 31 (Hong Kong High Court), when considering a claim against an assistant in a firm of solicitors. However, it should be emphasised that neither decision concerned an LLP. This diverging line of cases only raises issues in the case of negligence claims: in the case of other torts committed by a member, personal liability is almost inevitable: see, in particular, the Limited Liability Partnerships Act 2000, s.6(4).

NOTE 20. See now the Income Tax (Trading and Other Income) Act 2005, s.862, which, save as to corporation tax, replaces the Income and Corporation Taxes Act 1988, s.118ZA (as itself now amended by *ibid.* Sch.1, para.97).

Formation of an LLP

2–38 NOTE 27. The Companies Act 1985, s.242, in its application to LLPs, has been prospectively further amended by the Limited Liability Partnerships (Amendment) Regulations 2005 (SI 2005/1989), Sch.1, para.10.

NOTE 30. Schs 1 and 3 are prospectively amended by the Limited Liability Partnerships (Amendment) Regulations 2005, Schs 1, 2.

Winding up

2–41 NOTE 47. The Insolvency Act 1986, s.122(1), in its application to LLPs, has been prospectively further amended by the Limited Liability Partnerships (Amendment) Regulations 2005, Sch.2, para.6.

CHAPTER 3

GENERAL NATURE OF A PARTNERSHIP

1. The Commercial and Legal Views

The legal view

The first sentence of Lord Lindley's formulation was approved by the Supreme   **3–04**
Court of Canada in *Backman v. R*, 3 I.T.L. Rep. 647, at [41].

NOTE 5. See also *Byford v. Oliver* [2003] E.M.L.R. 20 at [26]; *Wan v. General
Commissioners for Division of Doncaster*, 76 T.C. 211. And note *BP Oil UK Ltd
v. Lloyds TSB Bank plc* [2005] 3 E.G. 116 (CS), CA (although this brief report
does not disclose that the three companies were originally partners).

NOTE 8. See also *Hiskett v. The Now Dissolved Firm of G & G Wilson*, 2003
G.W.D. 38–1036, OH.

2. Status of Firm in Specific Contexts

(a) Firm name

Effect of change in partners

Employees of firm

The decision of the Court of Appeal in *Rose v. Dodd*, *The Times*, August 16, 2005   **3–13**
should also be noted in this context. See further, *infra*, paras 25–02, 25–03.

NOTE 31: See now *Stevens v. Bower* [2004] I.R.L.R. 957, CA, which places the
matter beyond doubt.

NOTE 32. The *obiter* views expressed by Beldam J. in *Jeetle v. Elster* [1985]
I.C.R. 389 were approved by the Court of Appeal in *Stevens v. Bower, supra*,
where the partnership had been dissolved by reason of illegality and the business
carried on by the sole remaining qualified "partner".

Passing off

3–18 *Byford v. Oliver* [2003] E.M.L.R. 20 is an interesting example of the principles discussed in this paragraph. There it was held that individual former members of the heavy metal band "Saxon", which was a partnership at will and had long since been dissolved, had no right to the name and, thus, could not claim that a subsequent band adopting that name were guilty of passing off. The position might have been otherwise if the claim had been made by or on behalf of the dissolved partnership, unless its right to the name could properly be regarded as having been abandoned.

NOTE 54. See also *Sir Robert McAlpine Ltd v. Alfred McAlpine Plc* [2004] R.P.C. 36.

Firm name as a trade mark

3–19 NOTE 62. In *Byford v. Oliver, supra,* two former members of the band "Saxon" had sought to register the name, but it was, in the event, held that they were prohibited from doing so by *ibid.* ss.3(6) (bad faith) and 5(4) (use liable to be prevented by the law of passing off).

NOTE 64. See also *Byford v. Oliver, supra.* Also, see now *Kerly's Law of Trade Marks and Trade Names* (14th ed.), paras 9–150 *et seq.*

3–20 NOTE 69. See now *Kerly's Law of Trade Marks and Trade Names* (14th ed.), paras 13–059 *et seq.*

(d) Partnership Disabilities

Disabilities of one partner affect the firm

3–42 NOTE 40. Equally, if there is *no* disability affecting the partner in question, it is unlikely to be inferred that there is a disability affecting his firm: *Malkinson v. Trim* [2003] 1 W.L.R. 463.

Conflicts of interest

3–43 NOTE 43. *Koch Shipping Inc v. Richards Butler* is now reported at [2002] 2 All E.R. (Comm) 957. See also *Ball v. Druces & Attlee* [2002] P.N.L.R. 23 and [2004] P.N.L.R. 39; *Marks & Spencer Group plc v. Freshfields Bruckhaus Deringer* [2004] 1 W.L.R. 2331.

NOTE 46. See also *Hilton v. Barker Booth & Eastwood* [2005] 1 W.L.R. 567. Note that, in *Burkle Holdings v. Laing* [2005] EWHC 638 (QB), it was held that, where a solicitor acts for two parties to a transaction, professional privilege will only be available if there is a written retainer for *each* client: see L.S.G. May 26, 2005, p.6. This would seem to be at odds with the recognition in *Ball v. Druces & Attlee, supra,* that a retainer may be express or implied.

(f) Revenue Law

Effect of change in the firm

Partners are now each regarded as carrying on a *notional* trade (as opposed to a   **3–52**
deemed trade) under the Income Tax (Trading and Other Income) Act 2005,
s.852.

CHAPTER 4

CAPACITY OF PARTNERS

1. CAPACITY

(a) Aliens

Effects of war

4–05 Note that, for this principle to apply, a state of war must exist in the *technical* sense: see *Ahmed Amin v. Brown, The Times*, August 24, 2005.

NOTE 21. See also *Ahmed Amin v. Brown, supra.*

(c) Persons Suffering from Mental Disorder

4–13 NOTE 60. See, generally, *Masterman-Lister v. Jewell* [2003] 3 All E.R. 162, CA.

NOTE 61. See also *infra*, para.24–27.

(d) Husbands and Wives

Partnerships between husband and wife

4–17 It is now clear that, in an appropriate case, HM Revenue & Customs will seek to treat such a partnership as involving a settlement under the Income Tax (Trading and Other Income) Act 2005, ss.620, 624, 625: see, *infra*, para.34–12A. By way of contrast, in *Robertson v. Robertson*, 2003 S.L.T. 208, OH, it was held that a partnership agreement was not a marriage settlement and, thus, could not be varied under the Family Law (Scotland) Act 1985.

(f) Bankrupts and Disqualified Persons

4–23 Note that the Insolvency Act 1986, s.360(1) now also applies to a discharged bankrupt who is subject to a bankruptcy restriction order: *ibid.* subs.(5), as added by the Enterprise Act 2002, Sch.21, para.3.

NOTE 89. The prescribed amount is now £500: see the Insolvency Proceedings (Monetary Limits) (Amendment) Order 2004 (SI 2004/547).

(g) Trustees, Personal Representatives and Nominees

Nominees

NOTE 3. *cf.* the position where a nominee holds shares in a company: see *Re* **4–27**
Brightview Ltd [2004] 2 B.C.L.C. 191, at [31], [36]–[38].

2. THE SIZE RESTRICTIONS

All statutory restrictions on the size of partnerships were removed by the **4–30**
Regulatory Reform (Reform of 20 Member Limit in Partnerships etc.) Order *et seq.*
2002 (SI 2002/3203), reg.2, with effect from December 21, 2002.

CHAPTER 5

RULES FOR ASCERTAINING THE EXISTENCE OF A PARTNERSHIP

1. GENERAL OBSERVATIONS

Partnership Act 1890, section 2

5–02 As from a day to be appointed, the words ", widower, surviving civil partner" will be added after "widow" in the Partnership Act 1890, s.23(3)(c) by the Civil Partnership Act 2004, Sch.27, para.2.

Joint ventures

5–07 NOTE 17. See also *Small v. Fleming*, 2003 S.C.L.R. 647, OH, at [40]. Having described a joint venture as a "species of partnership", Lord Macfadyen went on to hold that a joint venture could not exist in the absence of agreement on all the terms. This seems odd, given the very general requirements of the Partnership Act 1890, s.1(1), to which he specifically referred.

NOTE 24. See also *Ness Training Ltd v. Triage Central Ltd*, 2002 S.L.T. 675, OH.

NOTE 25. See also *Ness Training Ltd v. Triage Central Ltd*, *supra*.

2. CO-OWNERSHIP

Co-owners not necessarily partners

5–08 A more recent illustration of the principle is to be found in *Pratt v. Medwin*, September 20, 2002 (Lawtel 2/10/2002), where the original two parties, Messrs Pratt and Medwin, had over a period acquired three properties for renovation and use in their insurance broking business and/or for letting. Mr Medwin subsequently transferred his share in one property to his son. Sonia Proudman Q.C., sitting as a deputy judge of the Chancery Division, held that no partnership existed and this issue was not pursued on the appeal.

Co-ownership and partnership compared

NOTE 35. This was regarded as a factor of some significance in *Pratt v. Medwin*, *supra*. **5–09**

NOTE 44. The National Health Service (General Medical Services) Regulations 1992 have now been revoked by the General Medical Services and Personal Medical Services Transitional and Consequential Provisions Order 2004 (SI 2004/865). See, as to the current payment regime, the National Health Service Act 1977, s.28T (as added by the Health and Social Care (Community Health and Standards) Act 2003, s.175(1)) and the National Health Service (General Medical Services Contracts) Regulations 2004 (SI 2004/291), reg.22.

4. SHARING PROFITS

(a) Sharing Profits as Evidence of Partnership

Loans and other agreements where no sharing of losses

It will often be argued by one party that a transaction was, on a true analysis, one **5–28**
of loan not of partnership. Thus, in *Chahal v. Mahal*, September 30, 2004 (Lawtel 5/10/04), Mr Chahal had provided the sum of £30,000 towards a particular venture, which represented more than twice the value of his house and part of which was raised by means of a bank loan. Hazel Williamson Q.C., sitting as a deputy judge of the Chancery Division, held that it was unlikely that such a sum had been loaned on an unsecured and interest-free basis (see *ibid.* at [67], [70]) and ultimately held that a partnership existed. The existence of the partnership was not challenged on appeal at [2005] EWCA Civ 898 (Lawtel 18/7/05). A different attitude may, however, be taken in the case of arrangements between members of the same family: see *Mehra v. Shah*, August 1, 2003 (Lawtel 5/8/03), where a loan, again of £30,000, had been made by one sister to her brothers and, on the evidence fell to be treated as such: see *ibid.* [33], *per* Sonia Proudman Q.C., sitting as a deputy judge of the Chancery Division. The overall finding of no partnership was upheld on appeal at [2004] EWCA Civ 632 (Lawtel 20/5/04).

NOTE 5. And note *Chahal v. Mahal*, *supra*, at [79] to [81]. **5–30**

5. PARTNERSHIP BY ESTOPPEL

(a) Holding Out

Form and time of representation

Merely opening a bank account in a business name is unlikely to amount to a **5–47**
sufficient representation for this purpose: *Elite Business Systems UK Ltd v. Price* [2005] EWCA Civ 920 (Lawtel 6/9/05).

Knowingly suffering a holding out

5–49 An attempt to rely on an *unauthorised* representation in a so-called registration form was, predictably, unsuccessful in *Elite Business Systems UK Ltd v. Price*, *supra*.

(b) Reliance

5–52 The decision in *Nationwide Building Society v. Lewis* should be contrasted with that in *Sangster v. Biddulph* [2005] P.N.L.R. 33. On a somewhat similar set of facts, Etherton J. held that the claimant *had* relied on the presence of a second "partner" when instructing the firm.

(c) The Giving of Credit

5–56 NOTE 88. See also *Sangster v. Biddulph, supra*, at [17], [18].

Salaried partners

5–70 Further examples of the divergent nature of the authorities are to be found in two recent decisions of the Employment Appeal Tribunal. In *Bower v. Hughes Hooker & Co.*, March 27, 2003, it was held that the salaried partner was a true partner, even though he did not contribute capital or bear a share of any losses. The determinative factor appears to have been the extent of his participation in the management of the firm. This aspect was not pursued on the appeal sub nom. *Stevens v. Bower* [2004] I.R.L.R. 957. On the other hand, in *Farrell Matthews & Weir v. Hansen* [2005] I.C.R. 509, the Tribunal appears to have accepted without question that the salaried partner was merely an employee.

Fixed share partners

5–70A It should be noted that, in an attempt to distance themselves from the overtones of employment which are so often associated with salaried partnership, many firms now resort to the alternative status of "fixed share partner", denoting a partner who is principally remunerated by a fixed share of profits. Intrinsically, this is no different from the more traditional salaried partnership, but as a result of the *de facto* requirements which HM Revenue & Customs expect to be satisfied before partner status is accepted, the following attributes are now shared by most fixed share partners:

> (a) entitlement to a small share of residual profits and losses (over and above their fixed profit shares);
>
> (b) an obligation to contribute a small sum of capital; and
>
> (c) a right to participate, to a greater or lesser extent, in the decision-making process of the firm.

In the current editor's view, none of these attributes are truly determinative of partnership status. What is, ultimately, far more important is to ensure that such a partner's fixed share is payable only out of profits and not irrespective of the firm's profitability: a "partner" who is remunerated even when the firm makes a loss is much more likely to be treated as an employee. See also para.10–81.

CHAPTER 6

CONSIDERATION FOR A CONTRACT OF PARTNERSHIP

Medical partnerships in the National Health Service

The National Health Service Act 1977, s.54 has been further amended by the **6–05**
Health and Social Care (Community Health and Standards) Act 2003, Sch.11,
para.26 and *ibid.* Sch.10 has been further amended by the Health and Social Care
Act 2001, s.14(3) and the Health and Social Care (Community Health and
Standards) Act 2003, Sch.11, para.43. A further prohibition on the sale of
goodwill by various types of contractors and certain medical practitioners providing "essential services" is also to be found in the Primary Medical Services (Sale
of Goodwill and Restrictions on Sub-contracting) Regulations 2004 (SI
2004/906), reg.3(1).

CHAPTER 7

EVIDENCE BY WHICH A PARTNERSHIP MAY BE PROVED

3. PARTNERSHIPS GENERALLY

(b) How is it to be Proved

Usual evidence of partnership

7–30   (i) *Accounts*

NOTE 81. See also, as to the evidential value of accounts, *Mehra v. Shah*, August 1, 2003 (Lawtel 5/8/2003) at [37], [38], *per* Sonia Proudman Q.C., sitting as a deputy judge of the Chancery Division. This evidence was, however, not pivotal on the appeal at [2004] EWCA Civ 632, at [27] (Lawtel 20/5/2004). And note *Abbott v. Price* [2003] EWHC 2760 (Ch), at [89] (Lawtel 26/11/03).

7–31   (iv) *Agreements and other documents*

NOTE 95. See also, as to the adoption of a draft agreement, *Thakrar v. Vadera*, March 31, 1999 (unreported), a decision of Arden J. *Cf. Abbott v. Price, supra*, at [75].

7–32   (ix) *Joint bank accounts*

NOTE 3. Note also, as to the absence of a joint account, *Kings v. King* [2004] S.T.C. (SCD) 186, 198.

CHAPTER 8

ILLEGAL PARTNERSHIPS

1. WHICH PARTNERSHIPS ARE ILLEGAL

Illegality never presumed

The distinction between a contract which is illegal *ab initio* and a contract the **8–02**
performance of which subsequently involves an incidental act of illegality was
clearly drawn by the Court of Appeal in *Colen v. Cebrian (UK) Ltd*, *The Times*,
November 27, 2003. And note also *Hall v. Woolston Hall Leisure Ltd* [2001] 1
W.L.R. 225, CA.

Competition

(A) ARTICLE 81 E.C.

NOTE 11. Note also, in this context, *Volkswagen AG v. Commission of the* **8–05**
European Communities (T208/01) [2004] I.C.R. 1197.

(C) ENTERPRISE ACT 2002

A partnership formed in order to facilitate or commit a "cartel offence" under **8–06A**
ibid. s.188 would clearly be illegal, since such an offence connotes positive
dishonesty on the part of the participants in promoting the proscribed arrangement in relation to two or more undertakings: see *ibid.* s.118(1), (2). For this
purpose the expression "undertaking" has the same meaning as in the Competition Act 1998: Enterprise Act 2002, s.188(7). However, it is difficult to conceive
of circumstances in which such a partnership might be contemplated.

Discrimination

Sexual discrimination. Although s.11 of the Sex Discrimination Act 1975 states **8–08**
in terms that it is unlawful for "a firm" to discriminate against a woman, etc., it
appears likely that, in applying the section, the Employment Tribunal will seek

to ensure that the partner discriminated against, even though a member of that firm, will not bear a share of any compensation awarded. This is a logical extension of the decision of the Employment Appeal Tribunal in *Dave v. Robinska* [2003] I.C.R. 1248. There one partner had dissolved the partnership on the grounds of the other's pregnancy. She sought to maintain that the Employment Tribunal did not have jurisdiction to hear the applicant partner's claim because she alone, as the other partner, could not constitute "a firm". That argument was rejected, it being held that s.11(1) should be given a wide interpretation and that the reference to "the firm" could include not only the *other* members of a three- or more partner firm but also one member of a two-partner firm. The same result would be achieved even if one looked at the position following the dissolution. However, the current editor submits that the decision leaves too many unanswered questions if applied in the context under consideration. What if one of four partners dissolved the firm by reason of a partner's pregnancy? Why should the remaining two innocent partners, who would be powerless to prevent the dissolution, be liable along with the partner guilty of the act of discrimination? This scarcely seems an attractive result. Inexplicably, the same result would not be achievable in the case of discrimination by an LLP, since it is doubted that the reference to the firm in subs.(6) could be read as referring to the other members of the LLP; *sed quaere*. Moreover, the *obiter* assumption on the part of the Tribunal that, where a majority of partners decide to commit an unlawful act of discrimination, the complainant can proceed against *all* the other partners seems highly questionable. It should also be noted that the decision in *Mair v. Wood*, 1948 S.C. 83 (see, further, para.20–11) was not cited to the Tribunal. Permission to appeal was given but no appeal has been reported at the time of writing.

An example of the type of conduct which may lead to a complaint of discrimination is to be found in *Sinclair Roche & Temperley v. Heard* [2004] I.R.L.R. 763 (EAT), albeit that the original decision of the Employment Tribunal was set aside and remitted for a rehearing. *Semble*, there may even be an unlawful act of discrimination after the partnership has been terminated, whether by virtue of a dissolution, retirement, expulsion or otherwise. The legislation has been construed liberally in the case of an employee (see *Relaxion Group Plc v. Rhys-Harper* [2003] I.C.R. 867, HL) and it seems reasonable to assume that a similar approach would be adopted in the present context, even allowing for the difference in wording, *i.e.* "a position as a partner" would *prima facie* include a former position as such.

It should be noted that, as from October 1, 2005, it will also be unlawful for a firm to harass a woman who holds or has applied for the position of a partner in the firm in relation to that position: Sex Discrimination Act 1986, s.11(2A), as added by the Employment Equality (Sex Discrimination) Regulations 2005 (SI 2005/2467), reg.14(2).

NOTE 27. *Dave v. Robinska*, *supra*, demonstrates that a power to dissolve the firm will be regarded as a power of expulsion for this purpose. It should be noted that the Sex Discrimination Act 1975, s.82(1A)(b) also refers to

"the termination of that person's . . . partnership by any act of his (including the giving of notice) in circumstances such that he is entitled to terminate it without notice by reason of . . . the conduct of the other partners".

This would seem to contemplate a case of repudiation and acceptance, but it is now clear that the doctrine of repudiation has no application to partnerships: see *infra*, paras 24–05 *et seq. Quaere*, do these words perhaps refer to a partner's right to obtain a dissolution under the Partnership Act 1890, s.35? This seems unlikely. It is inconceivable that the agreement would entitle a partner to terminate his partnership *without* any form of notice whatsoever.

NOTE 30. As from October 1, 2005, this exception will cease: see the Employment Equality (Sex Discrimination) Regulations 2005, reg.14(3).

NOTE 31. Note that the Sex Discrimination Act 1975, ss.7B(2) and 11(3C) will not, as from a day to be appointed, apply in the case of discrimination against a person who holds a full gender recognition certificate issued under the Gender Recognition Act 2004, s.9: *ibid.* ss.7A(4), 11(3D), as added by the Gender Recognition Act 2004, Sch.6, paras 3, 5.

Racial discrimination. Section 10 of the Race Relations Act 1976 has been amended by the Race Relations Act 1976 (Amendment) Regulations 2003 (SI 2003/1626), reg.12. The same issues as canvassed, *supra*, para.8–08 will also arise in this context. **8–09**

Disability discrimination. The Disability Discrimination Act 1995 has now been applied to all partnerships irrespective of their size: see *ibid.* ss.6A to 6C, as added by the Disability Discrimination Act 1995 (Amendment) Regulations 2003 (SI 2003/1673), reg.6. The applicable provisions are, to all intents and purposes, identical to those contained in the Sex Discrimination Act 1975 and it follows that the same issues noted, *supra*, para.8–08 will again arise. The expression "disability" is defined in the Disability Discrimination Act 1995, Sch.1, as prospectively amended by the Disability Discrimination Act 2005, s.18, Sch.1, Pt 1, para.36, Sch.2. In certain circumstances, it may be incumbent on the firm to make adjustments to accommodate a partner's disability: *ibid.* s.6B. As to the likely scope of this duty, note *Archibald v. Fife Council* [2004] I.C.R. 954, HL (albeit a case concerning an employee).

Religious or belief-based discrimination. It is now unlawful for a firm (see, *supra*, para.8–08) to discriminate against a partner or prospective partner on the grounds of his or her religion or beliefs: see the Employment Equality (Religion or Belief) Regulations 2003 (SI 2003/1660), reg.14. Again the form of the legislation follows that of the Sex Discrimination Act 1975 and similar issues will arise. **8–09A**

Sexual orientation-based discrimination. It is also unlawful for a firm (again see, *supra*, para.8–08) to discriminate against a partner or prospective partner on the grounds of his or her sexual orientation: see the Employment Equality (Sexual Orientation) Regulations 2003 (SI 2003/1661), reg.14. Again the form of the legislation follows that of the Sex Discrimination Act 1975 and similar issues will arise.

Age discrimination. Discrimination on the grounds of age is due to be outlawed as from October 2006, although the final form of the legislation is not yet known.

Nevertheless, it seems overwhelmingly likely that it will be applied to partnerships in the same way as other discrimination legislation. The default national age of retirement thereunder will be 65.

Statutory grounds of illegality

Accountants

8–17 NOTE 71. The reference in the first line should be to the Companies Act 1989, Sch.11. Note that *ibid.* s.30, Sch.11, Pt III have been amended/added by the Companies (Audit, Investigations and Community Enterprise) Act 2004, s.2, Sch.2, Pt 1, para.2.

Bankers

8–18 NOTE 80. See also the following Financial Services and Markets Act 2000 (Regulated Activities) (Amendment) Orders: SI 2002/682, 2002/1776, 2003/1475, 2003/1476, 2003/2822, 2004/1610, 2004/2737, 2005/593, 2005/922 and 2005/1518.

Bookmakers

8–19 Bookmaker's permits under the Betting, Gaming and Lotteries Act 1963 will, as from a date to be appointed, be replaced by operating licences under the Gambling Act 2005, Pt 5. A partnership may be a licensee thereunder: see *ibid.* s.80(5)(b). Failure to hold a licence to carry on the relevant activity will result in the commission of an offence under *ibid.* s.33. At the time of writing no regulations have been made under the Act.

Consumer credit businesses

8–20 to 8–27 All functions required to be performed by the Director General of Fair Trading under the Consumer Credit Act 1974 are now performed by the Office of Fair Trading (OFT): see the amendments contained in the Enterprise Act 2002, Sch.25, para.6. For ease of reference, this point will not be referred to further.

8–27 NOTE 16. The Consumer Credit Act 1974, s.37(1)(c) is prospectively amended by the Mental Capacity Act 2005, Sch.6, para.21.

NOTE 18. The Consumer Credit Act (Termination of Licences) Regulations 1976 have been further amended by the Consumer Credit Act 1974 (Electronic Communications) Order 2004 (SI 2004/3236), reg.3(2).

Dentists

8–28 NOTE 25. Note that this section was amended by the Medical Act 1983 (Amendment) Order 2002 (SI 2002/3135), Sch.1, Pt I, para.11 and is prospectively further amended by the Dentists Act 1984 (Amendment) Order 2005 (SI 2005/2011), art.34.

NOTE 26. This section is prospectively further amended by the Dentists Act 1984 (Amendment) Order 2005, art.35.

NOTE 27. This section is prospectively amended by the Health and Social Care (Community Health and Standards) Act 2003, Sch.11, para.50, Sch.14, para.4.

NOTE 28. This section is prospectively amended by the Civil Partnership Act 2004, Sch.27, para.89 and the Dentists Act 1984 (Amendment) Order 2005, art.37.

NOTE 31. The Dentists Act 1984, s.24 is prospectively amended and ss.25 and 27 are substituted by the Dentists Act 1984 (Amendment) Order 2005, arts 11, 12 and 18 respectively.

NOTE 29. This section is prospectively amended by the Dentists Act 1984 (Amendment) Order 2005, art.36.

Estate agents

All functions required to be performed by the Director General of Fair Trading **8–30** under the Estate Agents Act 1979 are now performed by the Office of Fair Trading (OFT): see the amendments contained in the Enterprise Act 2002, Sch.25, para.9.

The size restrictions on partnership between estate agents were removed by the Regulatory Reform (Reform of 20 Member Limit in Partnerships etc.) Order 2002 (SI 2002/3203), reg.2, with effect from December 21, 2002.

Financial services

NOTE 45. See also the following Financial Services and Markets Act 2000 **8–31** (Regulated Activities) (Amendment) Orders: SI 2002/682, 2002/1776, 2003/1475, 2003/1476, 2003/2822, 2004/1610, 2004/2737, 2005/593, 2005/922 and 2005/1518.

NOTE 47. See also the Financial Services and Markets Act 2000 (Exemption) (Amendment) Order 2003 (SI 2003/47), the Financial Services and Markets Act 2000 (Exemption) (Amendment) (No.2) Order 2003 (SI 2003/1675) and the Financial Services and Markets Act 2000 (Exemption) (Amendment) Order 2005 (SI 2005/592).

NOTE 49. Note, in this context, *CR Sugar Trading Ltd v. China National Sugar & Alcohol Group Corp* [2003] 1 Lloyd's Rep. 279 (a decision under the Financial Services Act 1986, s.5).

NOTE 58. This section has been amended by the Insurance Mediation Directive **8–32** (Miscellaneous Amendments) Regulations 2003 (SI 2003/1473), reg.9.

NOTE 60. See also Financial Services and Markets Act 2000 (Designated Professional Bodies) (Amendment) Order 2004 (SI 2004/3352).

8–33 NOTE 67. Note also the Financial Services and Markets Act 2000 (Variation of Threshold Conditions) Order 2001 (SI 2001/2507); the Financial Services and Markets Act 2000 (Variation of Threshold Conditions) Order 2002 (SI 2002/2707); and the Financial Services and Markets Act 2000 (Variation of Threshold Conditions) (Amendment) Order 2005 (SI 2005/680).

8–36 NOTE 89. Note that the Insolvent Partnerships Order 1994, art.19(4) has been further amended by the Insolvent Partnerships (Amendment) (No.2) Order 2002 (SI 2002/2708), art.5.

8–37 These restrictions were removed by the Regulatory Reform (Reform of 20 Member Limit in Partnerships etc.) Order 2002 (SI 2002/3203), reg.2, with effect from December 21, 2002.

Medical practitioners

8–38 The Medical Act 1983, s.46(1) will, as from a date to be appointed, apply the stated prohibition to any person who is not fully registered *and who does not hold a licence to practice*: see the Medical Act 1983 (Amendment) Order 2002 (SI 2002/3135), art.12(4). The licensing regime will be contained in a new Pt IIIA of the 1983 Act, as prospectively added by *ibid.* art.10. It will be an offence under that regime to pretend to hold a licence: Medical Act 1983, s.49A, as prospectively added by *ibid.* art.12(7).

8–39 It is, moreover, now clear that, subject to compliance with certain conditions, a partnership comprising at least one medical practitioner and one or more unqualified persons will be recognised under the National Health Service and may enter into a general medical services contract with a Primary Care Trust: see the National Health Service Act 1977, s.28S, as added by the Health and Social Care (Community Health and Standards) Act 2003, s.175(1); and see also the General Medical Services (Transitional Measure Relating to Non-Clinical Partners) Order 2004 (SI 2004/1772).

NOTE 96. The National Health Service Act 1977, s.54 has been further amended by the Health and Social Care (Community Health and Standards) Act 2003, Sch.11, para.26 and *ibid.* Sch.10 has been further amended by *ibid.* Sch.11, para.43. A further prohibition on the sale of goodwill by various types of contractors and certain medical practitioners providing "essential services" is also to be found in the Primary Medical Services (Sale of Goodwill and Restrictions on Sub-contracting) Regulations 2004 (SI 2004/906), reg.3(1).

NOTE 97. This regulation has now been revoked. An equivalent provision is not to be found in the National Health Service (General Medical Services Contracts) Regulations 2004 (SI 2004/291).

Patent and trade mark agents

8–40 All size restrictions were removed by the Regulatory Reform (Reform of 20 Member Limit in Partnerships etc.) Order 2002 (SI 2002/3203), reg.2, with effect from December 21, 2002.

NOTE 3. This footnote should refer to the Trade Marks Act 1994, ss.84(2), 85, regarding the use by firms of the designation "registered trade mark agents". Also, as to registration as such, see *ibid*. s.83. The Register of Trade Mark Agents Rules 1990 and the Registered Trade Mark Agents (Mixed Partnerships and Bodies Corporate) Rules 1994 remain in force, both having effect as if made under the 1994 Act.

Solicitors

For another instance in which a solicitors' partnership was dissolved by reason **8–41** of illegality on a partner being struck off the roll of solicitors, see *Bower v. Hughes Hooker & Co*, March 27, 2003, EAT (the issue was not pursued further on appeal: see *Stevens v. Bower* [2004] I.R.L.R. 957, CA). The position is the same in the case of an intervention by the Law Society in the firm's practice: see *Rose v. Dodd, The Times*, August 16, 2005 (and Lawtel 27/7/05), CA (albeit that the views expressed by the Court were strictly *obiter*). The bankruptcy of a partner will have the same effect, since it will, as in the case of an intervention, result in automatic suspension of his practising certificate.

NOTE 7. The European Communities (Lawyer's Practice) Regulations 2000 have been further amended by the European Communities (Lawyer's Practice) (Amendment) Regulations 2004 (SI 2004/1628).

NOTE 8. And note the decision in *R v. The Master of the Rolls* [2005] 2 All E.R. 640.

Notwithstanding what is said in the final sentence, where a partner is struck off **8–42** the roll of solicitors such a situation may still arise: see *Bower v. Hughes Hooker & Co, supra*.

All restrictions on the size of firms were removed by the Regulatory Reform **8–43** (Reform of 20 Member Limit in Partnerships etc.) Order 2002 (SI 2002/3203), reg.2, with effect from December 21, 2002.

Stockbrokers

As in the case of solicitors (see *supra*, para.8–43), all size restrictions have now **8–44** been removed.

NOTE 26. See also the following Financial Services and Markets Act 2000 (Regulated Activities) (Amendment) Orders: SI 2002/682, 2002/1776, 2003/1475, 2003/1476, 2003/2822, 2004/1610, 2004/2737, 2005/593, 2005/922 and 2005/1518.

Unregistered partnerships, etc.

All statutory restrictions on the size of partnerships were removed by the **8–45** Regulatory Reform (Reform of 20 Member Limit in Partnerships etc.) Order 2002 (SI 2002/3203), reg.2, with effect from December 21, 2002.

Veterinary surgeons

8–46 NOTE 33. See also the Veterinary Surgery (Rectal Ultrasound Scanning of Bovines) Order 2002 (SI 2002/2584); the Veterinary Surgery (Artificial Insemination of Mares) Order 2004 (SI 2004/1504); the Veterinary Surgery (Vaccination against Foot-And-Mount Disease) Order 2004 (SI 2004/2780); and the Veterinary Surgery (Testing for Tuberculosis in Bovines) Order 2005 (SI 2005/2015). The Veterinary Surgeons' Qualifications (EEC Recognition) Order 1980, art.5(1) has been revoked and replaced by the Veterinary Surgeons' Qualifications (European Recognition) Order 2003 (SI 2003/2919), art.10(1).

NOTE 37. The Veterinary Surgeons' Qualifications (EEC Recognition) Order 1980, art.5(9)(b) has been revoked and replaced by the Veterinary Surgeons' Qualifications (European Recognition) Order 2003, art.10(9)(b).

2. CONSEQUENCES OF ILLEGALITY

8–47 For other examples, also involving solicitors' partnerships, see *Bower v. Hughes Hooker & Co*, March 27, 2003, EAT (this issue not being pursued on appeal: see *Stevens v. Bower* [2004] I.R.L.R. 957) and *Rose v. Dodd, The Times*, August 16, 2005 (and Lawtel 27/7/05), CA.

Actions between members of an illegal partnership

8–53 NOTE 59. See also *Pickering v. Deacon, The Times*, April 19, 2003, CA.

Other examples: bookmaking partnerships

8–62 Note that the statutory regime governing such partnerships will, as from a date to be appointed, change: see, *supra*, para.8–19.

CHAPTER 9

DURATION OF PARTNERSHIP

The normal rule: partnership at will

NOTE 4. See also *Thakrar v. Vadera*, March 31, 1999 (unreported), a decision of **9–03** Arden J.

Express and implied agreements negativing partnership at will

The fact that a partnership agreement remains in draft does not necessarily mean **9–05** that its terms have not been adopted as binding, particularly if the partners have subsequently agreed to amend those terms: see *Thakrar v. Vadera*, March 31, 1999 (unreported), a decision of Arden J.

NOTE 15. See also *Thakrar v. Vadera, supra.*

Part Two

FORMATION OF PARTNERSHIP BY FORMAL AGREEMENT

CHAPTER 10

PARTNERSHIP AGREEMENTS

1. CONSTRUCTION AND APPLICATION OF PARTNERSHIP AGREEMENTS

A. AGREEMENT CONSTRUED IN THE FACTUAL MATRIX

10–04   NOTE 18. See also *P and S Platt Ltd v. Crouch, The Times*, August 27, 2003, CA; *Stroude v. Beazer Homes Ltd, The Times*, April 28, 2005, CA.

B. AGREEMENT CONSTRUED BY REFERENCE TO THE PARTNERS' OBJECTIVES

10–05   *Thakrar v. Vadera*, March 31, 1999, unreported, exemplifies this principle. There Arden J. had to construe an agreement which included provision that

> "The termination of the Partnership with regard to a Partner shall terminate the Partnership with regard to the remaining Partners".

She nevertheless held that the partnership was not a partnership at will.

C. WORDS AND DOCUMENTS GIVEN THEIR NATURAL AND ORDINARY MEANING

10–06   A recent example of this principle is to be found in *Ellis v. Coleman*, December 10, 2004 (Lawtel 10/12/04), where Lawrence Collins J. had no hesitation in holding that an arbitration clause was equally applicable to continuing and outgoing partners, even though on its face it appeared to be limited merely to "partners".

NOTE 34. See also *Folkes Group Plc v. Alexander* [2002] 2 B.C.L.C. 254.

NOTE 36. See also *Egan v Static Control Components (Europe) Ltd* [2004] 2 Lloyd's Rep. 429, CA; *Sirius International Insurance Co (Publ) v. FAI General Insurance Ltd* [2004] 1 W.L.R. 3251, HL.

NOTE 37. See also *Folkes Group PLC v. Alexander, supra.*

10–07   NOTE 39. Also *cf. Folkes Group Plc v. Alexander, supra.*

G. TERMS IMPLIED TO GIVE THE AGREEMENT BUSINESS EFFICACY

10–11   Partnership agreements increasing contain "entire agreement" clauses, but these may not be effective to exclude implied terms: see *Exxonmobil Sales and Supply Corp v. Texaco Ltd* [2004] 1 All E.R. (Comm) 435. See also *infra*, para.10–12.

NOTE 52. And see also *Times Newspapers Ltd v. George Weidenfeld & Nicolson Ltd* [2002] F.S.R. 29; *Northern and Shell Plc v. John Laing Construction Ltd*, 90 Con. L.R. 26, noticed *infra*, para.10–37; *Townends Group Ltd v. Cobb, The Times*, December 1, 2004.

H. TERMS VARIED BY EXPRESS OR IMPLIED AGREEMENT

Express agreement

Where such a power is exercised in accordance with its terms, it does not matter **10–13** that some partners will suffer an incidental disadvantage, unless that was the sole purpose of the exercise (when the majority would, almost by definition, not be acting in good faith): see, generally, *Redwood Master Fund Ltd v. TD Bank Europe Ltd*, *The Times*, January 30, 2003 (relating to decisions taken under a syndicated loan agreement).

NOTE 63. See also *Hole v. Garnsey* [1930] A.C. 472, 496 (*per* Lord Atkin), cited in Blackett-Ord's *Partnership* (2nd ed.) at para.7–20.

NOTE 65. Note, however, the observations of the Court of Appeal in *Chahal v. Mahal* [2005] EWCA Civ 898 (Lawtel 18/7/05), at [40]; to a similar effect were views expressed by Etherton J. in *Ashborder BV v. Green Gas Power Ltd* [2004] EWHC 1517 (Ch), (Lawtel 14/7/04), at [227] (albeit a decision relating to the construction and application of a company debenture).

Implied agreement

As to the difficulties which may be experienced in establishing the adoption of **10–14** a term by virtue of an implied agreement, see *Summers v. Smith*, March 27, 2002 (Lawtel 2/4/02). Such an implication may also be difficult to draw where the agreement contains an "entire agreement" clause: see *North Sea Ventilation Ltd v. Consafe Engineering (UK) Ltd*, July 20, 2004 (Lawtel 4/10/04), at [27] (*per* H.H. Judge Cockcroft sitting as a deputy judge of the High Court), citing *Inntrepreneur Pub Co (GL) v. East Crown Ltd* [2000] 2 Lloyd's Rep. 611, at [7] (*per* Lightman J.). Similarly, where the agreement requires all variations to be in writing, although the partners may be shown to have dispensed with this requirement.

2. STATUTORY INTERFERENCE WITH CONTRACTUAL RIGHTS

To the list of impermissible acts of discrimination must now be added discrimina- **10–26** tion on the grounds of a partner or prospective partner's disability (Disability Discrimination Act 1995, s.6A (as added by the Disability Discrimination Act 1995 (Amendment) Regulations 2003 (SI 2003/1673), reg.6), religion or belief (Employment Equality (Religion or Belief) Regulations 2003 (SI 2003/1660), reg.14) or sexual orientation (Employment Equality (Sexual Orientation) Regulations 2003 (SI 2003/1661), reg.14). Discrimination on the grounds of age will also be unlawful as from 2006. See further, *supra*, para.8–09A.

When dealing with a public company, it may also be necessary to inquire whether it is within the powers of the directors to agree to enter into an agreement containing certain terms, *e.g.* a so-called "poison pill" provision: see *Criterion Properties Plc v. Stratford Properties LLC* [2004] 1 W.L.R. 1846, HL.

10–27 It is clear that the horizontal effect of the Human Rights Act 1998 is still the subject of much debate: see *X v. Y (Employment Sex Offender)* [2004] I.C.R. 1634, CA. In that case, it was held that the Act *may* in certain circumstances be engaged in disputes between private employers and employees under the statutory regime established by the Employment Rights Act 1996. Might a similar argument be deployed in the case of, say, an application for a dissolution under s.35 of the Partnership Act 1890? Although the scope for involving the 1998 Act is naturally limited, the current editor believes that this possibility cannot be entirely ruled out.

10–28 In *Robertson v. Robertson*, 2003 S.L.T. 208, OH, it was, perhaps predictably, held that a partnership agreement was not a marriage settlement and, thus, could not be varied under the Family Law (Scotland) Act 1985.

3. USUAL CLAUSES FOUND IN A PARTNERSHIP AGREEMENT

C. COMMENCEMENT DATE

Retrospective and future commencement dates

10–37 The retrospectivity of an agreement depends on the parties' intentions which may be apparent from the terms of the agreement or may be implied as a matter of business efficacy, having regard to the factual matrix: see *Northern and Shell Plc v. John Laing Construction Ltd*, 90 Con. L.R. 26, at [51] to [54], [58], CA.

D. DURATION

10–39 On occasion a "rolling" term may be adopted, which can give rise to difficulties of construction in terms of when the partnership can be brought to an end. Note, in this context, *G & A Ltd v. HN Jewelry (Asia) Ltd* [2004] EWCA Civ 674 (Lawtel 27/5/04), albeit that this did not concern a partnership agreement.

G. PARTNERSHIP PREMISES

Premises owned by one or more partners

10–44 See generally, as to implied occupation rights between partners and their termination following a dissolution (albeit on an interim application), *Latchman v. Pickard* [2005] EWHC 1011 (Ch) (Lawtel 12/5/05).

It should be noted that such premises may now be deemed to be partnership property for the purposes of the stamp duty land tax regime introduced by the Finance Acts 2003 and 2004: see *infra*, para.38–15. As a result a charge to the tax may be incurred when they "become" partnership property: see *infra*, para.38–16.

H. Partnership Property

NOTE 85. A note of the appeal in *Swift v. Dairywise Farms Ltd* now appears at **10–46** [2003] 1 W.L.R. 1606.

Land

The transfer of land into a partnership may now attract a charge to stamp duty **10–49** land tax, as introduced by the Finance Acts 2003 and 2004: see *infra*, para.38–16.

Outgoing partners

NOTE 5. See also *Customs & Excise Commissioners v. Allen* [2003] B.P.I.R. 830. **10–51** Such an order cannot, however, be retrospective: *Darrell v. Miller* [2004] B.P.I.R. 470.

I. Income and Liabilities Derived From Previous Business

It is considered that the assumption of a share of existing partnership liabilities **10–55** will not, in general, amount to consideration in money or money's worth for the acquisition of an incoming partner's share for stamp duty land tax purposes, save perhaps where such debts are secured on land owned by the firm: see *infra*, para.38–17.

In the case of a solicitors' firm, the "new" firm created by the admission of partner will, almost inevitably, be a successor practice within the meaning of Appendix 1 to the current Solicitors' Indemnity Insurance Rules: see (2005) L.S.G., March 24, p.19.

NOTE 16. See further, as to the position in Scotland, *Ocra (Isle of Man) Ltd v. Anite Scotland Ltd*, 2003 S.L.T. 1232, OH.

L. Books and Accounts

Preparation of annual (or other) accounts

NOTE 63. Note, however, that the basis on which partnership accounts are drawn **10–72** up has now changed: see *infra*, para.21–04.

Agreed accounts not binding for all purposes

Cf. Gadd v. Gadd [2002] 08 E.G. 160 and *Champion v. Workman*, June 20, 2001 **10–74** (Lawtel 22/8/01), noticed, *infra*, para.10–159.

M. PROFITS AND LOSSES

Profit sharing arrangements

10–78 As regards the profit sharing arrangement listed in sub-para.(c), *i.e.* the traditional "lockstep", account must be taken of the potential impact of the proposed age discrimination legislation due to be introduced in 2006. Although the extent of that impact is not yet clear, it seems unlikely that a pure lockstep approach to profit sharing will be permissible.

NOTE 91. Note that in *Chartered Accountants' Firm v. Braisby* [2005] S.T.C. (SCD) 389, an agreed adjustment to an outgoing partner's profit share unusually caused the continuing partners' "salaries" to be of a negative amount. It was held that this did not matter, since such salaries only represent a method of arriving at the allocation of profits.

"Salaried" and "fixed share" partners

10–81 See further, as to the *de facto* requirements imposed by HM Revenue & Customs as a condition of recognition as a fixed share partner, *supra*, para.5–70A.

Medical partnerships within the National Health Service

10–82 The Secretary of State is now charged with the duty of policing the statutory prohibitions on the sale of goodwill, in place of the Medical Practices Committee. Whether the same approach as formerly adopted by that Committee continues to be applied is unclear.

NOTE 11. The National Health Service Act 1977, s.54 has been further amended by the Health and Social Care (Community Health and Standards) Act 2003, Sch.11, para.26, and *ibid.* Sch.10 has been further amended by *ibid.* Sch.11, para.43. A further prohibition on the sale of goodwill by various types of contractors and certain medical practitioners providing "essential services" is also to be found in the Primary Medical Services (Sale of Goodwill and Restrictions on Sub-contracting) Regulations 2004 (SI 2004/906), reg.3(1).

Division of profits

10–84 It should be noted that the decision to divide profits (in contradistinction to the manner in which they are to be shared between the partners once divided) will be a management decision unless the agreement provides otherwise: see *Stevens v. South Devon Railway Co* (1851) 9 Hare 313, 326, *per* Sir G.J. Turner V.-C.; also *Burland v. Earle* [1902] A.C. 83, 95.

Tax and other provisions

10–85 *Tax provisions*

NOTE 20. But see now the Income Tax (Trading and Other Income) Act 2005, ss.848 *et seq.* See *infra*, paras 34–04 *et seq.*

Other provisions

Workman v. Champion, June 20, 2001 (Lawtel 22/8/01), is one of the rare cases **10–86** where the propriety of making a provision as against a retiring partner has been considered by the court. There the provision was allowed, even though there was evidence that the claim in question had been settled for a lesser amount: see *ibid.* at [43], [44] (*per* Lawrence Collins J.).

N. POWERS AND DUTIES OF PARTNERS

Restrictions on the authority of partners

NOTE 54. See also *Mahon v. Sims, The Times*, June 16, 2005 (a restrictive **10–95** covenant case).

P. RETIREMENT

(a) Voluntary retirement

NOTE 80. As from October 1, 2005, the Sex Discrimination Act 1975, s.11(4) will **10–104** cease to apply: see the Employment Equality (Sex Discrimination) Regulations 2005, reg.14(3).

(b) Compulsory retirement on grounds of age

As from 2006, new age discrimination legislation will be introduced. It is clear **10–109** that this will apply equally to partners as to employees.

Q. EXPULSION

(a) Powers of Expulsion

Grounds for expulsion

NOTE 11. In *Thakrar v. Vadera*, March 31, 1999, an unreported decision of Arden **10–111** J., a ground was framed by reference to a partner committing "a serious breach of any of the provisions of this deed resulting in the partnership's suffering a material disadvantage". It was held that the acts complained of were not sufficient.

NOTE 13. Such a ground was relied on, albeit unsuccessfully, in *Thakrar v. Vadera, supra.*

Dishonesty etc. Note that there are three possible standards of dishonesty which **10–114** may be applied in any given case: see *Twinsectra Ltd v. Yardley* [2002] 2 A.C. 164, at [27] (*per* Lord Hutton). *Semble* the subjective test will not be apposite in the present context. In the current editor's view, the objective test will in most cases be applicable and little or no scope will be left for the so-called "combined" test. *Sed quaere. Cf. infra*, para.16–07.

10–116 *Discretionary grounds:* To this list should now be added discrimination on the grounds of disability (Disability Discrimination Act 1995, s.6A (as added by the Disability Discrimination Act 1995 (Amendment) Regulations 2003 (SI 2003/1673), reg.6)), religion or belief (Employment Equality (Religion or Belief) Regulations 2003 (SI 2003/1660), reg.14) or sexual orientation (Employment Equality (Sexual Orientation) Regulations 2003 (SI 2003/1661), reg.14). Discrimination on the grounds of age will also be unlawful as from 2006. See further, *supra*, para.8–09A.

NOTE 32. As from October 1, 2005, the Sex Discrimination Act 1975, s.11(4)(a) will cease to apply: see the Employment Equality (Sex Discrimination) Regulations 2005, reg.14(3).

Construction of expulsion clauses

10–119 In *Thakrar v. Vadera, supra*, the decision in *Re A Solicitors' Arbitration* was held to be of no relevance to the construction of a power of expulsion exercisable in a two partner firm.

NOTE 48. *Thakrar v. Vadera, supra*, is another example, albeit less compelling as there were only two partners.

Exercise of the power

10–120 The motive for the purported expulsion was addressed by Arden J. in *Thakrar v. Vadera, supra*.

10–121 As to discrimination, see *supra*, para.10–116.

NOTE 56. As from October 1, 2005, the Sex Discrimination Act 1975, s.11(4)(b) will cease to apply: see the Employment Equality (Sex Discrimination) Regulations 2005, reg.14(3).

Compliance with strict terms of expulsion clause

10–122 In *Thakrar v. Vadera, supra*, it was held that a meeting had to be convened, as required by the power in question, even though there were only two partners.

Effect of invalid expulsion notice

10–126 NOTE 82. For an analogous decision on invalidity, see *Concord Trust v. The Law Debenture Trust Corporation Plc* [2004] 2 All E.R. (Comm) 737, CA (which concerned a notice given under a trust deed).

Remedies for wrongful expulsion

10–127 There would seem to be no reason in principle why a partner who is wrongfully expelled should not also recover damages for loss of reputation: see *Mullins v. Laughton* [2003] Ch. 250, at [128] to [131] (*per* Neuberger J.).

Note 89. Interestingly, in *Thakrar v. Vadera*, *supra*, the service of an invalid expulsion notice was not, seemingly, regarded as material by Arden J. when ordering a dissolution under the Partnership Act 1890, s.35(f) (the just and equitable ground).

Repudiation by wrongful expulsion

It is now clear that this is no longer a legally tenable argument: see *infra*, paras **10–128**
24–05, 24–06.

(b) Powers of Compulsory Retirement, etc.

Note 3. As from October 1, 2005, the Sex Discrimination Act 1975, s.11(4) will **10–130**
cease to apply: see the Employment Equality (Sex Discrimination) Regulations
2005, reg.14(3).

(c) Acquisition of Expelled/Retired Partner's Share

A further variation on this theme is the so-called "poison pill" provision con- **10–133**
sidered in *Criterion Properties Plc v. Stratford UK Properties LLC* [2004] 1
W.L.R. 1846, HL, *i.e.* a right for one partner to insist that another buys out his
share in the firm. Needless to say, such provisions are unusual.

R. Power to Dissolve Firm

(a) General Power

Effect of invalid dissolution notice

It is now clear that service of an invalid dissolution notice cannot constitute a **10–136**
repudiatory breach: see *infra*, paras 24–05, 24–06.

S. Garden Leave and Related Matters

Validity of garden leave clauses

In *Goodchild v. Chadwick*, September 18, 2002 (unreported), Kevin Garnett Q.C. **10–144**
(sitting as a deputy judge of the Chancery Division) declined to grant an interim
injunction enforcing a garden leave clause on the grounds that the claimants were
unlikely to suffer any loss of business, but the validity of the clause was not
called into question.

Note 59. Note also *TFS Derivatives Ltd v. Morgan* [2005] I.R.L.R. 246.

[37]

T. THE OUTGOING PARTNER'S FINANCIAL ENTITLEMENT

(a) Manner of Acquisition

10–147 Note also the so-called "poison pill" provision considered in *Criterion Properties Plc v. Stratford Properties LLC* [2004] 1 W.L.R. 1846, HL. See *supra*, para.10–133.

10–149 NOTE 91a. See also *Fraser v. Oystertec Plc* [2004] B.C.C. 233.

10–150 NOTE 96. And see also, as to the statutory purpose required to invoke *ibid.* s.423, *I.R.C. v. Hashmi* [2002] 2 B.C.L.C. 489, CA.

(c) Quantifying the Amount due to the Outgoing Partner

10–154 NOTE 24. As from October 1, 2005, the Sex Discrimination Act 1975, s.11(4)(a) will cease to apply: see the Employment Equality (Sex Discrimination) Regulations 2005, reg.14(3).

Outgoing partner's share of surplus assets

10–155 NOTE 26. Note, in this context, that the required basis for drawing up partnership accounts has now changed: see *infra*, para.21–04. And see, as to the valuation of work in progress on dissolution in the case of a solicitors' firm, *Finlayson v. Turnbull (No.4)*, 2003 G.W.D. 12–374, OH.

(3) *Book or Balance Sheet Value*

10–159 *Gadd v. Gadd* [2002] 08 E.G. 160 is a more recent instance in which the court favoured a market value approach, albeit emphasising, consistently with the decision of the Court of Appeal in *Re White*, that the construction of the partnership deed is paramount. Equally, in *Champion v. Workman*, June 20, 2001 (Lawtel 22/8/01), Lawrence Collins J. held that, on the true construction of a deed effecting the retirement of a partner, where accounts had to be prepared as at a certain date, they should be prepared on the same basis as previous accounts of the firm and should not adopt a different approach in valuing work in progress.

10–165 *Relevance of past conduct: Gadd v. Gadd, supra*, is a case of this class. There accounts had been drawn up for some time prior to the date of death showing the property in question at its historic cost. Jules Sher Q.C. (sitting as a deputy judge of the Chancery Division) held that, in drawing up those accounts, the partners had not concentrated on the difference between historic costs and market value. This should be contrasted with the decision in *Champion v. Workman, supra*.

The basis of valuation: fair or market value?

10–170 Market value was the expression used in *Gadd v. Gadd, supra*.

Special balance sheet to be drawn up

Cf. Champion v. Workman, supra.   **10–173**

NOTE 22. See also, as to the effect of departure by an expert from his instructions,   **10–174**
Veba Oil Supply & Trading GmbH v. Petrotrade Inc [2002] 1 All E.R. 703,
CA.

(e) Annuities to Outgoing Partners, Widows, etc.

NOTE 34. As from April 6, 2006, these sections will be repealed by the Finance   **10–177**
Act 2004, Sch.42, Pt 3 and replaced by the new pension regime introduced under
ibid. Pt 4.

Discontinuance of business

NOTE 45. For a recent illustration of a similar principle being applied in the case   **10–181**
of a commercial contract, see *CEL Group Ltd v. Nedlloyd Lines UK Ltd* [2004]
1 All E.R. (Comm) 689, CA.

Contracts (Rights of Third Parties) Act 1999

NOTE 53. Note, as to disapplying the Act, *Nisshin Shipping Co Ltd v. Cleaves &*   **10–185**
Co Ltd [2004] 1 Lloyd's Rep. 38.

U. GOODWILL AND RESTRICTIONS ON COMPETITION

(a) Meaning of Goodwill

Firm name

NOTE 77. See *Byford v. Oliver* [2003] E.M.L.R. 20, noticed *infra*,   **10–192**
para.10–198.

(b) Ownership of Goodwill

(1) *Dissolution of firm*

Use of firm name following dissolution

In *Byford v. Oliver* [2003] E.M.L.R. 20 it was held that individual former   **10–198**
members of the heavy metal band "Saxon" had no right to the firm name
following a dissolution of their partnership at will, but that the dissolved firm
might be in a position to assert rights thereto, subject to questions of abandonment, etc. Laddie J. distinguished the decision in *Burchell v. Wilde* [1900] 1 Ch.
551, holding that it laid down no rule of general application. The key factor was,
ultimately, that the former partners had not actually used the name following the
dissolution and, accordingly, had not acquired any proprietary interest of their
own in that name. Had they done so, the position might well have been
different.

(c) Valuation of Goodwill

Goodwill treated as valueless

10–213   NOTE 72. The National Health Service Act 1977, s.54 has been further amended by the Health and Social Care (Community Health and Standards) Act 2003, Sch.11, para.26 and *ibid.* Sch.10 has been further amended by *ibid.* Sch.11, para.43. A further prohibition on the sale of goodwill by various types of contractors and certain medical practitioners providing "essential services" is also to be found in the Primary Medical Services (Sale of Goodwill and Restrictions on Sub-contracting) Regulations 2004 (SI 2004/906), reg.3(1).

(d) Restrictions on Competition

Enforceability of restrictions

10–218   *Quaere*, could it be argued that a restriction on competition is invalidated if it breaches an outgoing partner's right of freedom of establishment in another Member State under Art.43 EC? There might be some scope for such an argument since Art.43 does have horizontal effect as between private parties (see *Viking Line Abp v. International Transport Workers' Federation*, *The Times*, June 22, 2005), although the instances in which it could be invoked will be rare.

Note also, in this context, the potential implications of the decision in *Days Medical Aids Ltd v. Pihsiang Machinery Manufacturing Co Ltd* [2004] 1 All E.R. (Comm) 991, noticed *infra*, para.10–236.

(1) *Reasonableness in the Interests of the Parties*

Legitimate interest capable of protection

10–222   If the agreement seeks to define the interest to be protected, it is unlikely to be possible to justify the restraint by reference to some other interest: see *Office Angels Ltd v. Rainer-Thomas* [1991] I.R.L.R. 214, at [39] (*per* Slade L.J.); *Countrywide Assured Financial Services Ltd v. Smart* [2004] EWHC 1214 (Ch) (Lawtel 7/5/04).

Restriction not excessive

10–225   In general, it will not be possible to supplement an express (and arguably invalid) restriction with an implied term (see *Townends Group Ltd v. Cobb*, *The Times*, December 1, 2004), save in the specific circumstances discussed in paras 10–204 *et seq.*

NOTE 25. See also *Deacons v. White & Case LLP* (HCA 2433/2002), October 24, 2003 Hong Kong High Court).

NOTE 35. See also *Days Medical Aids Ltd v. Pihsiang Machinery Manufacturing Co Ltd* [2004] 1 All E.R. (Comm) 991, which concerned the construction of a renewable distribution agreement alleged to be in restraint of trade.

Note 38. See also *Arbuthnot Fund Managers v. Rawlings* [2003] EWCA Civ 518 **10–226**
(Lawtel 13/3/03); *TFS Derivatives Ltd v. Morgan* [2005] I.R.L.R. 246.

Note 40. See also *TFS Derivatives Ltd v. Morgan, supra.*

Note also the (ultimately inconclusive) analysis of the position by Cox J. in *TFS* **10–228**
Derivatives Ltd v. Morgan, supra.

(2) Reasonableness in the Interests of the Public

Note that the public interest featured prominently in the decisions in *Dranez* **10–229**
Anstalt v. Hayek [2003] 1 B.C.L.C. 278, CA, where a restriction was sought to
be imposed on a pioneer in the field of medical science, and *Leah Health Care
Services v. Deluca*, 2003 G.W.D. 32–892, Sh Ct, concerning an area restriction
imposed on an employee of a chiropractors' business.

Note 53. It *may*, nevertheless, be permissible to extend the restriction to all
employees in the case of a small firm with few employees: see *Hydra Plc v.
Anastasi* (2005) L.S.G., September 1, 23.

Severance

Note 65. For a recent example in which offending words were severed, see *TFS* **10–232**
Derivatives Ltd v. Morgan [2005] I.R.L.R. 246.

Injunctive relief

Note 71. See now *Snell's Equity* (31st ed.), paras 16–06 *et seq.* **10–234**

Note 72. See also *Centre for Maritime & Industrial Safety Technology Ltd v.
Crute*, 2003 G.W.D. 8–194, OH, where an injunction against an employee was
refused, in part on the basis that the client he was joining already had a subsisting
contractual relationship with his former employer.

Availability of an account

It is questionable to what extent an account of profits (as opposed to damages) **10–234A**
can be sought from a former partner who breaches a valid restriction on competition. In *WWF-World Wide Fund for Nature v. World Wrestling Federation
Entertainment Inc* [2002] F.S.R. 504 at [63], Jacob J. held that an account was not
available in restraint of trade cases, but the possibility was left open by Mance
L.J. in *Experience Hendrix LLC v. PPX Enterprises Inc* [2003] 1 All E.R.
(Comm) 830, at [32]. See also *ibid.* at [55], *per* Peter Gibson L.J. A former
partner is no longer in a fiduciary relationship with the continuing partners, so
this would not be a material factor.

Penalties and liquidated damages

Quaere whether an arrangement under which an outgoing partner is obliged to **10–235**
account to the continuing partners for a percentage of the actual fees earned from

work carried out on behalf of former clients of the firm during a specified period following his retirement would be regarded as a penalty, particularly if the percentage significantly exceeds the profit costs likely to be derived from such work. Although the current editor considers the point to be arguable, account must also be taken of the overhead burden assumed by the continuing partners, *e.g.* where existing staff are retained but are, in the event, underemployed.

NOTE 75. See now *Chitty on Contracts* (29th ed.), paras 26–109 *et seq.*

Article 81 E.C.

10–236 It should be noted that the operation of the restraint of trade doctrine may be abrogated in a case which would, but for an applicable exemption or because it would not affect trade between Member States, fall within the ambit of Art.81: see *Days Medical Aids Ltd v. Pihsiang Machinery Manufacturing Co Ltd* [2004] 1 All E.R. (Comm) 991.

NOTE 86. See further *Crehan v. Inntrepreneur Pub Co (CPC)* [2004] 3 E.G.L.R. 128, CA; also *Provimi Ltd v. Roche Products Ltd* [2003] 2 All E.R. (Comm) 683.

Competition Act 1998

10–240 NOTE 15. See also, *supra*, para.10–236, n.86.

10–242 Individual exemptions are no longer available with the repeal of s.4 by the Competition Act 1998 and Other Enactments (Amendment) Regulations 2004 (SI 2004/1261), Sch.1, para.2. Similarly in the case of ss.12 to 16: *ibid.* Sch.1, para.9.

NOTE 27. Nor, as significantly, will it be invalidated under the restraint of trade doctrine: see, *supra*, para.10–236.

Enterprise Act 2002: cartel offences

10–242A Although this Act introduced the concept of a "cartel offence" in relation to arrangements affecting one or more undertakings (see *ibid.* s.188), the offence can only be committed by individuals and a primary ingredient is actual dishonesty. In the circumstances, it is doubted whether this will have any direct impact on partnership arrangements.

V. PROVISIONS CONSEQUENTIAL ON THE DEATH, RETIREMENT OR
EXPULSION OF A PARTNER

(a) Assignment of Outgoing Partner's Share, etc.

Stamp duty land tax

10–246 An assignment of a partnership share in return for a consideration in money or money's worth will now in most cases be chargeable to stamp duty land tax under the Finance Act 2003, Sch.15 (as amended by the Finance Act 2004, Sch.41), to the extent that the partnership property consists of land or an interest in land, irrespective of whether a document effecting that assignment is brought into existence: see *infra*, para.38–19. In certain circumstances, the withdrawal of balances due to an outgoing partner will be treated as consideration for these purposes: *ibid.* It now seems clear that the old stamp duty regime will no longer have any application in such circumstances, where the partnership property consists of assets other than land: see *infra*, para.38–13.

(b) Indemnity to Outgoing Partner

Effect of indemnity

NOTE 64. Equally, a part payment by one of the continuing partners will clearly restart the limitation period running as against the outgoing partner *qua* surety: *UCB Corporate Services Ltd v. Kohli* [2004] 2 All E.R. (Comm) 422.   **10–249**

W. ADMISSION OF NEW PARTNERS

Rule 1

NOTE 95. As to whether the application of the Act is excluded by a contrary intention, see *Nisshin Shipping Co Ltd v. Cleaves & Co Ltd* [2004] 1 Lloyd's Rep. 38.   **10–256**

X. WINDING UP

Division of assets in specie

A division of assets *in specie* following a dissolution is seemingly likely to lead to a charge to stamp duty land tax in all cases, even where the division directly reflects the former partners' shares in the partnership: see *infra*, para.38–21. And see *infra*, para.A6–32, regarding value added tax.   **10–261**

NOTE 16. See also the following additional cases concerning the ability of a solicitor to act against his former client: *Koch Shipping Inc v. Richards Butler* [2002] 2 All E.R. (Comm) 957; *Ball v. Druces & Attlee* [2002] P.N.L.R. 23 and [2004] P.N.L.R. 39; *Marks & Spencer Group plc v. Freshfields Bruckhaus Deringer* [2004] 1 W.L.R. 2331.   **10–262**

Y. ARBITRATION AND MEDIATION

(a) Arbitration

NOTE 38. An option in favour of one party to insist on disputes being referred to arbitration may, if exercised, amount to an arbitration agreement for this purpose: **10–267** see *NB Three Shipping Ltd v. Harebell Shipping Ltd* [2005] 1 All E.R. (Comm) 200. *Cf.* the position where one party has the option to litigate the matter in court and, thus, to override the arbitration agreement: *Law Debenture Trust Corp v. Elektrim Finance BV, The Times*, August 4, 2005. Note also, in this context, the exceptional decision in *Flight Training International Inc v. International Fire Training Equipment Ltd* [2004] 2 All E.R. (Comm) 568.

NOTE 43. However, general words of incorporation may not suffice: *Excess Insurance Co Ltd v. Mander* [1995] I.R.L.R. 358; *Trygg Hansa Insurance Co Ltd v. Equitas and Butcher* [1998] 2 Lloyd's Rep. 439.

NOTE 45. Repudiation of a *partnership* agreement is no longer possible (see *infra*, para.24–05 *et seq.*), but this does not mean that an arbitration agreement contained therein might not, in appropriate circumstances, be repudiated. If an arbitration agreement *is* repudiated, it will no longer be enforceable: see *Downing v. Al Tameer Establishment* [2002] 2 All E.R. (Comm) 545, CA. Note that a repudiation argument failed in *Indescon Ltd v. Ogden* [2005] B.L.R. 152. Illegality of the main agreement is another example of a case falling within this class: see *Vee Networks Ltd v. Econet Wireless International Ltd* [2005] 1 All E.R. (Comm) 303.

Persons bound by the arbitration agreement

10–268 NOTE 51. And see *Nisshin Shipping Co Ltd v. Cleaves & Co Ltd* [2004] 1 Lloyd's Rep. 38.

NOTE 54. *Semble*, the Arbitration Act 1996, s.82(2) will automatically effect this extension. See also *Schiffahrtsgesellschaft Detlev Von Appen GmbH v. Voest Alpine Intertrading GmbH* [1997] 2 Lloyd's Rep. 279, CA; *Through Transport Mutual Insurance Association (Eurasia) Ltd v. New India Assurance Co Ltd* [2005] 1 C.L.C. 376.

Scope of arbitration agreement

10–269 In *Ellis v. Coleman*, December 10, 2004 (Lawtel 10/12/04), Lawrence Collins J. held, perhaps predictably, that the expression "partners" in an arbitration clause extended not only to current but also to *former* partners in the firm.
The expression "dispute or difference" in an arbitration agreement is likely to be construed more widely than the word "dispute" appearing alone: *Amec Civil Engineering Ltd v. Secretary of State for Transport* [2005] 1 W.L.R. 2339, CA. And see also *Jagger v. Decca Music Group Ltd* [2005] F.S.R. 26.

Arbitration agreement generally no defence

10–270 NOTE 62. The views expressed in *Russell on Arbitration* (21st ed.), para.2–050, n.48 are not retained in the 22nd ed. at para.2–014.

NOTE 64. For a recent example of a *Scott v. Avery* clause, see *Jagger v. Decca Music Group Ltd*, *supra*.

Power of the court to order stay of proceedings

Equally, where proceedings are already on foot and one party seeks to introduce **10–271** an additional claim by amendment, it will be necessary to scrutinise the nature of the original claims to see whether that additional claim ought properly to be referred to arbitration at the insistence of that party. Thus, where the issue of a partner's misconduct and its implications was already raised in and central to the proceedings, it was held that a subsequent purported expulsion or dissolution arising out of the same facts ought properly to be heard by the court seised of those original issues: see *Ahad v. Uddin, The Times,* June 30, 2005, CA.

NOTE 74. The decision in *Birse Construction Ltd v. St David Ltd* was considered in *Al-Naimi v. Islamic Press Agency Inc* [2000] 1 Lloyd's Rep 522, CA; see also *Law Debenture Trust Corp v. Elektrim Finance BV, The Times,* August 4, 2005 (albeit that this aspect is not referred to in *The Times'* report).

NOTE 76. See also *Collins (Contractors) Ltd v. Baltic Quay Management (1994) Ltd* [2005] B.L.R. 63, CA. And note the exceptional decision in *Law Debenture Trust Corp v. Elektrim Finance BV, supra.*

NOTE 78. Note that the appeal in *Capital Trust Investments Ltd v. Radio Design TJ AB* was dismissed at [2002] 2 All E.R. 159.

NOTE 81. And see *T and N Ltd v. Royal and Sun Alliance Plc* [2002] EWHC 2420 **10–272** (Ch) (Lawtel 2/12/02); *El Nasharty v. J Sainsbury Plc* [2004] 1 Lloyd's Rep. 309; *Law Debenture Trust Corp v. Elektrim Finance BV, The Times,* August 4, 2005.

NOTE 87. See now *Russell on Arbitration* (22nd ed.), para.7–030.

Interim remedies

NOTE 88. As to the scope of the Arbitration Act 1996, s.43, note *BNP Paribas v.* **10–274** *Deloitte & Touche LLP* [2004] 1 Lloyd's Rep. 233. And see, as to orders for disclosure of documents, *Assimina Maritime Ltd v. Pakistan Shipping Corporation* [2005] 1 All E.R. (Comm) 460.

NOTE 89. The restriction of the court's powers save in cases of urgency under the Arbitration Act 1996, s.44(3) is a substantive fetter: see *Cetelem SA v. Roust Holdings Ltd* [2005] 2 All E.R. (Comm) 203, CA.

NOTE 99. See now *Russell on Arbitration* (22nd ed.), para.6–130. **10–276**

Appeals

NOTE 36. See also *Demco Investments & Commercial SA v. SE Banken Forsakr-* **10–281** *ing Holding Aktiebolag* [2005] EWHC 1398 (Comm) (Lawtel 13/7/05).

NOTE 40. See, for example, *CMA CGM SA v. Beteiligungs-KG MS "Northern Pioneer" Schiffahrtsgesellschaft mbH & Co* [2003] 1 W.L.R. 1015, CA.

Alternative Dispute Resolution

10–282 It is now clear that, as an alternative to a stay, a court may *order* parties to mediate their dispute: see *Shirayama Shokusan Co Ltd v. Danovo Ltd* [2004] B.L.R. 207.

NOTE 45. A party's refusal to mediate may, ultimately, be penalised in costs, but not in all cases: see for example, *Hurst v. Leeming* [2003] 1 Lloyd's Rep. 379.

NOTE 46. See also *Cable & Wireless plc v. IBM United Kingdom Ltd* [2002] 2 All E.R. (Comm) 1041.

Z. PENALTIES AND LIQUIDATED DAMAGES

10–283 NOTE 50. See now *Chitty on Contracts* (29th ed.), paras 26–109 *et seq.*

4. LIMITED LIABILITY PARTNERSHIP AGREEMENTS

10–284 NOTE 54. The potential application of *Williams v. Natural Life Health Foods Ltd* is considered further *supra*, para.2–37, n.18.

NOTE 59. It should, however, be noted that the Law Society has issued guidance to solicitors as to the use of the expression "partner" by members of a limited liability partnership: see (2005) L.S.G., June 16, p.39.

10–285 It would seem that inclusion of an arbitration clause in an LLP members' agreement is still desirable and may even permit the court to order a stay with a view to matters in dispute in connection with an application to wind up the LLP being referred to arbitration: see *Re Magi Capital Partners LLP* [2003] EWHC 2790 (Ch). A stay is less likely in the case of an application under the Companies Act 1985, s.459: see *Exeter City AFC Ltd v. Football Conference Ltd* [2004] 1 W.L.R. 2910 (which concerned a company).

CHAPTER 11

CORPORATE AND GROUP PARTNERSHIPS

1. THE CORPORATE PARTNERSHIP

Nature and formation

NOTE 1. See now the Solicitors' Incorporated Practice Rules 2004 and the **11–02** Solicitors' Indemnity Insurance Rules 2005, r.3(1).

Partnerships between "one man companies"

NOTE 12. And see also, as to the statutory purpose required to invoke *ibid.* s.423, **11–04** *I.R.C. v. Hashmi* [2002] 2 B.C.L.C. 489, CA.

Contents of corporate partnership agreement

In the case of an unusual term, such as a so-called "poison pill" provision, **11–09** whereby one partner is forced to buy the other out in certain eventualities (*e.g.* on a change in the former's management), it may be necessary to consider whether the directors have authority to authorise a corporate partner to enter into an agreement containing such a term, particularly in the case of a public company: see *Criterion Properties Plc v. Stratford UK Properties LLC* [2004] 1 W.L.R. 1846, HL.

Annual accounts

Note that these Regulations will, as from October 1, 2005, be amended by the **11–17** Partnerships and Unlimited Companies (Accounts) Amendment) Regulations 2005 (SI 2005/1987).

Part Three

THE RIGHTS AND OBLIGATIONS OF PARTNERS AS REGARDS THIRD PARTIES

CHAPTER 12

THE LIABILITY OF A PARTNER FOR THE ACTS OF HIS CO-PARTNERS

1. PARTNERS AS AGENTS

Partnership Act 1890, section 5

Analysis of the section

See further, as to the two limbs, *Bank of Scotland v. Henry Butcher & Co* [2003]   **12–03,**
2 All E.R. (Comm) 557, at [87] to [89], *per* Chadwick L.J.   **12–04**

Nature and ordinary course of business

Although the expressions "carrying on in the usual way business of the kind   **12–13**
carried on by the firm" in s.5 and "acting in the ordinary course of the business
of the firm" in s.10 (see para.12–94) differ, in substance they amount to the same
thing, as the Court of Appeal acknowledged in *J.J. Coughlan Ltd v. Ruparelia*
[2004] P.N.L.R. 4 at [2]. That said, whilst what is stated in the text remains
correct, the courts are, perhaps, more ready than they once were to find that a
partner was acting in the usual or ordinary course of the firm's business: see, for
example, *Dubai Aluminium Co Ltd v. Salaam* [2003] 2 A.C. 366, HL; *McHugh
v. Kerr* [2003] EWHC 2985 (Ch) (Lawtel 22/12/03), both decisions under s.10.
In cases of the latter type, vicarious liability brings clear policy considerations
into play: see *Dubai Aluminium Co Ltd v. Salaam, supra*, at [21], [22], *per* Lord
Nicholls and [107], *per* Lord Millett. This led Lord Nicholls to formulate the test
for liability under s.10 in these terms (*ibid.* at [23]):

> " . . . the wrongful conduct must be so closely connected with acts the partner . . . was
> authorised to do that, for the purpose of the liability of the firm . . . to third parties, the
> wrongful conduct may *fairly and properly* be regarded as done by the partner while
> acting in the ordinary course of the firm's business . . . ".

See also *ibid.* at [124] *per* Lord Millett. There is an obvious risk that this liberal
approach will in future colour the court's approach in cases falling within both

ss.5 and 10, as illustrated by Dyson L.J.'s observation in *J.J. Coughlan Ltd v. Ruparelia, supra*, at [30] that

" . . . the court should not be too ready to find that the ordinary business requirement is not satisfied."

Equally, it is fair to say that Dyson J. went on to recognise that the s.10 test formulated in *Dubai Aluminium* is "broader" (*ibid.* at [37]) but, on the facts, the court held that the fraud in question perpetrated by a solicitor in the course of promoting a "preposterous" and "abnormal" investment scheme did *not* satisfy the requirements of either section. Note also *Sweetman v. Nathan* [2004] P.N.L.R. 7, where the Court of Appeal allowed a negligence action brought against a solicitor's partners to proceed even though he had seemingly participated in a fraud jointly with the claimant. The court observed (at [66]) that

" . . . the plight of the innocent partners arouses sympathy but becoming a partner with a negligent or fraudulent person has as a consequence that you may be liable for his negligence or fraud."

In *McHugh v. Kerr* [2003] EWHC 2985 (Ch) (Lawtel 22/12/03), it was conceded that it was part of the ordinary business of "many firms of accountants" to buy and sell shares. The fact that the firm in question had, on occasion, done so put the matter beyond doubt: see *ibid.* at [42], *per* Lawrence Collins J.

Where a firm enters into a contract for the purposes of its business, any act required to be done pursuant to that contract will automatically be treated as done for such purposes and, thus, within the usual course of that business: *Bank of Scotland v. Henry Butcher & Co* [2003] 2 All E.R. (Comm) 557, CA. The same act, if done independently of the contract, may be treated differently: *ibid.*

Nevertheless, it may be that an act which actually brings the firm's business to and end (or which is clearly intended to have that effect) will not be regarded as done in the usual or ordinary course of its business: see *Chahal v. Mahal* [2005] EWCA Civ 898 (Lawtel 18/7/05), at [40] (albeit not a decision under ss.5 or 10 of the 1890 Act); also *Ashborder BV v. Green Gas Power Ltd* [2004] EWHC 1517 (Ch), (Lawtel 14/7/04), at [227], *per* Etherton J. (albeit a decision relating to the construction and application of a company debenture).

NOTE 28. Note, however, that this issue strictly involves a factual conclusion based on an assessment of the primary facts and may, to an extent, also involve a question of law: see *Dubai Aluminium Co Ltd v. Salaam, supra*, at [18], [24] (*per* Lord Nicholls) and [112] (*per* Lord Millett).

Solicitors' firms

12–14   The fact that the firm does little work in a particular area is *prima facie* irrelevant: *McHugh v. Kerr, supra*, at [43], *per* Lawrence Collins J.

12–15   The Court of Appeal's decision in *Dubai Aluminium Co Ltd v. Salaam* was reversed on appeal at [2003] 2 A.C. 366, and the firm was held liable for the partner's dishonest participation in the breach of trust which had, *inter alia,* involved the preparation of sham documents. Accordingly, all references to that decision should be qualified accordingly. Whilst sham documents had also been prepared in *J.J. Coughlan Ltd v. Ruparelia, supra*, the partner's conduct in this instance fell the other side of the line. Equally, if a fraudulent act in which both the solicitor and his client have colluded is, on a true analysis, independent of any breach of duty which he owes to his client, an action against his partners will still be maintainable: *Sweetman v. Nathan, supra*.

The question whether a solicitor might be said to be acting in the usual course of business by taking on a trusteeship, actual or constructive, was considered by the House of Lords in *Dubai Aluminium Co Ltd v. Salaam, supra*, at [40] to [42] (*per* Lord Nicholls) and [132] to [143] (*per* Lord Millett). In the light of their observations, it is submitted that the formulation in the text is still correct.

NOTE 41. *J.J. Coughlan Ltd v. Ruparelia, supra*, is another example of such a case.

The impact of changing business practices

Equally, it may be that changing business practices serve to *reinforce* decisions in earlier cases: see *Dubai Aluminium Co Ltd v. Salaam, supra*, at [134], where Lord Millett was considering the decisions in *Re Fryer* (1857) 3 K. & J. 317 and *Mara v. Browne* [1896] 1 Ch. 199. **12–16**

Commercial requirements of business

NOTE 48. See also *Bank of Scotland v. Henry Butcher & Co* [2003] 2 All E.R. (Comm) 557, CA, at [20] to [23], *per* Munby J. **12–17**

Scope of business

The scope of the firm's business may be defined by the terms of a contract into which it enters and, thus, authorise all acts required in connection with the contract's implementation, even if they would otherwise be outside the scope of that business: *Bank of Scotland v. Henry Butcher & Co, supra*. **12–19**

Admissions and representations

Partnership Act 1890, section 15

Equally, a representation made by an existing proprietor of a business does not bind persons with whom he subsequently enters into partnership, even if they relate to that proposed partnership: *In the matter of Burton Marsden Douglas* [2004] 3 All E.R. 222, at [30]. It was sought to be argued, unsuccessfully, that there had been a representation by silence *after* the partnership had been formed. **12–23**

Notice to partners

Firms with a common partner

NOTE 78. *Koch Shipping Inc v. Richards Butler* is now reported at [2002] 2 All E.R. (Comm) 957. See also *Ball v. Druces & Attlee* [2002] P.N.L.R. 23 and **12–27**

[2004] P.N.L.R. 39; *Marks & Spencer Group Plc v. Freshfields Bruckhaus Deringer* [2004] 1 W.L.R. 2331.

2. LIABILITY FOR ACTS WHICH ARE NOT IN THEMSELVES WRONGFUL

Actions

12–39   NOTE 5. Note, however, as to the ability of one partner to represent the firm in proceedings in Scotland, *Clark Advertising Ltd v. Scottish Enterprise Dunbartonshire* [2004] S.L.T. 85, Sh Ct.

Contracts

12–57   Equally, once a contract binding the firm has been entered into, any action to implement that contract will be authorised, even if it would otherwise fall outside the normal scope of a partner's authority: *Bank of Scotland v. Henry Butcher & Co* [2003] 2 All E.R. (Comm) 557, CA.

Deeds

Deed not necessary

12–68   NOTE 5. The point was also not considered by the Court of Appeal in *Bank of Scotland v. Henry Butcher & Co, supra.*

Executing partner bound

12–69   See also *Bank of Scotland v. Henry Butcher & Co, supra.*

Guarantees

12–72   It should be noted that a guarantee must be in writing, in order to comply with the requirements of s.4 of the Statute of Frauds 1677: *Actionstrength Ltd v. International Glass Engineering IN.GL.EN SpA* [2003] 2 A.C. 541, HL.

NOTE 18A. See now *Bank of Scotland v. Henry Butcher & Co* [2003] 2 All E.R. (Comm) 557, CA.

NOTE 21. See now *Bank of Scotland v. Henry Butcher & Co, supra.*

NOTE 23. See also *Bank of Scotland v. Henry Butcher & Co, supra.*

Insurance

12–75   Equally, a partner in a firm of solicitors has authority to enter into a professional indemnity insurance policy, which is required pursuant to the applicable Solicitors' Indemnity Insurance Rules: *Jones v. St Pauls International Insurance Co Ltd* [2004] EWHC 2209 (Ch) (Lawtel 23/4/04), at [12], *per* Hart J.

Trusts

See also *Dubai Aluminium Co Ltd v. Salaam* [2003] 2 A.C. 366, at [40] to [42]   **12–92**
(*per* Lord Nicholls) and [132] to [143] (*per* Lord Millett).

3. LIABILITY OF PARTNERS IN RESPECT OF TORTS, FRAUDS AND OTHER WRONGS

Partnership Act 1890, section 10

Scope of the section

In *Dubai Aluminium Co Ltd v. Salaam, supra,* the House of Lords endorsed the   **12–95**
Court of Appeal's view that the section extends beyond torts and other common
law wrongs and is equally capable of applying to equitable wrongdoing as well
as a breach of statute resulting in the imposition of a penalty. In the event it was
clearly held to apply in the case of dishonest participation in a breach of trust. See
further *supra*, para.12–13. Lord Millett (at *ibid.* [110]) appeared to reject any
perceived overlap between ss.10 and 11 (but note that the report of that paragraph
at [2002] 3 W.L.R. 1913, 1939 is inaccurate).

(a) Torts

NOTE 93. See also *Sweetman v. Nathan* [2004] P.N.L.R. 7, CA, noticed *supra*,   **12–98**
para.12–13. Although the firm may be vicariously liable for the act of negligence,
this does not mean that the firm *itself* has been negligent, should that be relevant:
see *Duncan v. Beattie*, 2003 S.L.T. 1243, OH.

(b) Frauds and Fraudulent Representations

For a recent illustration of a case in which the firm was held liable for a fraud   **12–101**
perpetrated by a partner in a firm of accountants, see *McHugh v. Kerr* [2003]
EWHC 2985 (Ch) (Lawtel 22/12/03).

NOTE 9. See also *MCI Worldcom International Inc v. Primus Telecommunications*   **12–102**
Inc [2004] 1 All E.R. (Comm) 138.

(c) Other Wrongs

The House of Lords' endorsement of the Court of Appeal's decision as to the   **12–110**
scope of s.10 in *Dubai Aluminium Co Ltd v. Salaam* [2003] 2 A.C. 366 has
already been noticed, *supra*, para.12–95. However, their Lordships declined to
uphold the decision that the partner's actions in dishonestly participating in the
breach of trust, though unauthorised by his co-partners, could not be said to have
been carried out in the ordinary course of the firm's business and thus held the
firm liable.

4. LIABILITY OF PARTNERS FOR MISAPPLICATION OF MONEY AND PROPERTY

Partnership Act 1890, section 11

NOTE 46. See also *Dubai Aluminium Co Ltd v. Salaam* [2003] 2 A.C. 366, at   **12–113**
[110], *per* Lord Millett.

NOTE 47. And also *Dubai Aluminium Co Ltd v. Salaam, supra*.

Section 11(b): Money or property in custody of firm

Group 2: Firm not liable

12–140   NOTE 4. See further *Dubai Aluminium Co Ltd v. Salaam* [2003] 2 A.C. 366, at [40] to [42] (*per* Lord Nicholls) and [132] to [143] (*per* Lord Millett).

5. LIABILITY OF PARTNERS FOR BREACHES OF TRUST

Partnership Act 1890, section 13

Interaction between sections 10 and 13

12–145   The decision in *Walker v. Stones* appears to have been endorsed by Lord Millett's analysis of the scope of ss.10 and 13 in *Dubai Aluminium Co Ltd v. Salaam, supra*, at [110], where he stated that

> "The innocent partners are not vicariously liable for the misappropriation, which will have occurred outside the ordinary course of business. But they are liable to restore the money if the requirements of the general law of knowing receipt are satisfied."

Where the section does not apply

Proviso (1): Notice of breach of trust

12–149   NOTE 29. See now *Dubai Aluminium Co Ltd v. Salaam, supra*, at [40] to [42] (*per* Lord Nicholls) and [132] to [143] (*per* Lord Millett).

NOTE 30. See *Dubai Aluminium Co Ltd v. Salaam, supra*.

7. LIABILITY OF PARTNERS IN RESPECT OF CONTRACTS IN IMPROPER FORM

(b) Contracts under Seal

The general rule

12–179   NOTE 1. See now *Bank of Scotland v. Henry Butcher & Co* [2003] 2 All E.R. (Comm) 557, CA.

CHAPTER 13

THE NATURE AND DURATION OF A PARTNER'S LIABILITY TO THIRD PARTIES

1. NATURE AND EXTENT OF THE LIABILITY

A. LIABILITY FOR ACTS WHICH ARE NOT IN THEMSELVES WRONGFUL

Partnership Act 1890, section 9

In *Dubai Aluminium Co Ltd v. Salaam* [2003] 2 A.C. 366, at [110] Lord Millett **13–03** observed that this section "is not concerned with the liability of the firm at all but with the liability of the individual partners." Note, however that the report of this paragraph at [2003] 3 W.L.R. 1913, 1939 is inaccurate.

B. LIABILITY IN RESPECT OF TORTS, FRAUDS AND OTHER WRONGS AND MISAPPLICATION OF MONEY AND PROPERTY

Partnership Act 1890, section 12

See, as to the distinction between the scope of the Partnership Act 1890, ss.10 **13–12** and 11, *Dubai Aluminium Co Ltd v. Salaam*, *supra*, at [110] *per* Lord Millett. As noted *supra*, para.13–03, the Weekly Law Reports version is inaccurate.

C. LIABILITY IN RESPECT OF BREACH OF TRUST

NOTE 42. See also *Dubai Aluminium Co Ltd v. Salaam*, *supra*, at [110] *per* Lord **13–13** Millett. As noted *supra*, para.13–03, the Weekly Law Reports version is inaccurate.

2. DURATION OF LIABILITY

A. COMMENCEMENT OF AGENCY

Incoming partners

13–24   The final sentence was cited with apparent approval by Lloyd J. in *In the matter of Burton Marsden Douglas* [2004] 3 All E.R. 222, at [28]. See also *ibid.* at [33].

New contract

13–27   See *In the matter of Burton Marsden Douglas*, *supra*, at [31], [32].

Agreement to take on existing debts

13–28   It should be noted that, in the case of a solicitors' partnership, the "new" firm may *de facto* be required to take on responsibility for insuring the "old" firm's liabilities, if (as will often be the case) it is regarded as a successor practice within the meaning of Appendix 1 to the current Solicitors' Indemnity Insurance Rules: see (2005) L.S.G., March 24, p.19.

NOTE 81. See further *Ocra (Isle of Man) Ltd v. Anite Scotland Ltd*, 2003 S.L.T. 1232, OH.

13–29   NOTE 83. See also *In the matter of Burton Marsden Douglas* [2004] 3 All E.R. 222, at [31].

Fraud on new partner

13–32   The final sentence of the first paragraph was cited with apparent approval by Lloyd J. in *In the matter of Burton Marsden Douglas*, *supra*, at [31].

B. TERMINATION OF AGENCY

Express revocation

Implied authority

13–36   But see now, as to the application of the doctrine of repudiation, *infra*, paras 24–05, 24–06.

Partnership Act 1890, sections 36 and 37

13–43   In *Hussein v. Commissioners of Customs & Excise* [2003] V. & D.R. 439, at [50], the VAT Tribunal held that the Commissioners of Customs & Excise were capable of being a person who "deals with a firm" within the meaning of s.36(1).

C. TERMINATION OF ACCRUED LIABILITY

(1) *Payment and Appropriation of Payments*

Appropriate of payments: the rule in *Clayton's Case*

Proposition 6:

Note that the application of the rule where monies are traced into a single account   **13–97**
is also doubtful: see *Commerzbank Aktiengesellschaft v. IMB Morgan Plc* [2005]
1 Lloyd's Rep. 298.

(2) *Release and Discharge*

Outgoing partner entitled to indemnity against debts, etc.

It follows that a part payment (but not an acknowledgement) by one of the   **13–104**
continuing partners will be effective as against the outgoing partner *qua* surety:
see *UCB Corporate Services Ltd v. Kohli* [2004] 2 All E.R. (Comm) 422,
applying the Limitation Act 1980, s.31(7), albeit not in the case of a
partnership.

(3) *Substitution of debtors and securities*

(A) SUBSTITUTION BY AGREEMENT

General principle

See also *In the matter of Burton Marsden Douglas* [2004] 3 All E.R. 222, at [31],   **13–107**
[32].

(C) LIMITATION

Continuing partnership

An acknowledgement of a partnership liability given by a partner in some other   **13–143**
capacity will naturally bind him in his capacity as a partner, as well as his
co-partners: *Harper v. John C Harper & Co (No.2)*, 2003 S.L.T. 102, Sh Ct.

Dissolved partnership

Note also the effect of a part payment or acknowledgment where an outgoing   **13–144**
partner has become a surety for the firm's obligations: see *supra*, para.13–104.

ACTIONS BY AND AGAINST PARTNERS

1. PARTIES TO ACTIONS AND RELATED MATTERS

A. ACTIONS IN FIRM NAME

Use of firm name in specific instances

Firm not liable

14–11 Similarly, where one firm's business is acquired by another but none of the former's partners join the acquiring firm. In *Kesslar v. Moore & Tibbits* [2005] P.N.L.R. 17, CA, the claimant had mistakenly issued proceedings against the latter but was, ultimately, permitted to substitute the partners in the acquired firm as defendants under CPR r.19.5(3)(a).

Merged firm

14–12 NOTE 26. *Cf. Kesslar v. Moore & Tibbits, supra.*

Service on firm

14–15 NOTE 38. The last known place of business of the firm denotes the last place known to the claimant: *Mersey Docks Property Holdings Ltd v. Kilgour* [2004] B.L.R. 412. The claimant or his advisers must, however, take reasonable steps to find out which is the firm's last place of business, if it cannot discover its current address: *ibid.* at [63].

D. CONDUCT OF ONE PARTNER AFFECTING FIRM'S RIGHTS

Actions against firm

14–68 Equally, where proceedings are commenced against one partner in respect of the affairs of his former firm but he defends the action through or in the name of his *current* firm, costs incurred by the latter are recoverable from the other party, just as if the partner were acting in person, even though, as between him and his co-partners, no costs are recoverable: *Malkinson v. Trim* [2003] 1 W.L.R. 463, CA.

3. SET-OFF

Lord Lindley's rules on set-off

NOTE 33. Note also, as to equitable set-off, *Benford Ltd v. Lopecan SL (No.2)* **14–78** [2004] 2 Lloyd's Rep. 618.

Part Four

THE RIGHTS AND OBLIGATIONS OF PARTNERS BETWEEN THEMSELVES

CHAPTER 15

MANAGEMENT AND DECISION MAKING

Disputes on ordinary matters

Rights of the minority

Where a majority have a power under the partnership agreement and exercise that **15–08** power in good faith, the fact that a minority of partners may be disadvantaged is not *per se* a ground for attacking the exercise of the power. *Per contra,* if the majority exercise the power *in order* to victimise or otherwise to disadvantage the minority: see, generally, *Redwood Master Fund Ltd v. TD Bank Europe Ltd*, *The Times*, January 30, 2003 (albeit a case relating to decisions taken under a syndicated loan agreement). See also *infra*, para.16–07.

CHAPTER 16

THE DUTY OF GOOD FAITH

1. THE NATURE OF THE DUTY

The general duty

16–01 There is a "duty to speak" even in the case of a joint venture agreement: see *Huyton SA v. Distribuidora Internacional de Productos Agricolas SA* [2004] 1 All E.R. (Comm) 402, CA. *Semble,* this duty will usually extend to disclosure by a partner of his own misconduct: see the discussion of the position of a director of a company in *Item Software (UJ) Ltd v. Fassihi* [2005] I.C.R. 450, CA; also *Tesco Stores Ltd v. Pook* [2004] I.R.L.R. 618 (as to the position of senior employees). Note also, in this context, *Connolly v. Brown*, 2004 G.W.D. 18–386, OH, where an agency relationship had arguably come to an end before the relevant information was acquired.

As to the effect of affirming an agreement, *e.g.* for retirement, with knowledge of a breach of duty by a partner, see also *Lindsley v. Woodfull* [2004] 2 B.C.L.C. 131, CA. This meant that the continuing partners had no right to an account going forward, although their accrued rights as to past breaches of duty were, in the circumstances, unaffected: see further *infra*, para.16–27.

The nature of the duty

16–03 See also *Deacons v. White & Case LLP* (HCA 2433/2002), October 24, 2003 (Hong Kong High Court).

16–04 Repudiation of a partnership contract in the *technical* sense (as opposed to the sense used by Lord Lindley) is no longer a relevant concept: see *infra,* paras 24–05 *et seq.*

Inchoate or dissolved partnerships

16–06 NOTE 20. *Per contra* where the proposed partners abandon their intention to form a partnership and decide to form a company instead: see *Ness Training Ltd v. Triage Central Ltd*, 2002 S.L.T. 675, OH.

Ingredients of a breach of the duty

Note the analysis of the three possible standards of dishonesty by Lord Hutton in   **16–07**
Twinsectra Ltd v. Yardley [2002] 2 A.C. 164, at [27]. In the present context, it
would appear that the combined objective/subjective test adopted in that case will
apply. *Cf.* the position under an expulsion clause requiring "dishonesty", noticed
supra, para.10–114.

It is doubted whether merely making preparations to set up a competing
business, *e.g.* acquiring premises or setting up a company which remains dormant, will without more breach the duty. In *Ward Evans Financial Services Ltd
v. Fox* [2002] I.R.L.R. 120, CA, the employment contracts specifically prohibited
the holding of an interest in a company which would impair the employees'
duties to act in the best interests of their employers, even if it remained dormant.
Much will, of course, depend on the precise facts: the more preparatory acts that
are carried out, the greater the chance of a breach of the duty of good faith.
British Midland Tool Ltd v. Midland International Tooling Ltd [2003] 2 B.C.L.C.
523 is an example of extreme conduct on the part of the directors of a company
(who were ultimately held to have been part of an unlawful means conspiracy).
See also *Deacons v. White & Case LLP, supra.*

Semble a partner is entitled to expect that any discretion conferred on the
management of the firm or on his fellow partners, *e.g.* under a performance-
related profit sharing scheme, will be exercised rationally and in good faith: see,
for an analogous example in the case of a contract of employment, *Horkulak v.
Cantor Fitzgerald International* [2005] I.C.R. 402, CA.

Equally, if a decision is *genuinely* taken (or a discretion exercised) in the best
interests of the firm, the fact that it may disadvantage a minority of the partners
is not *per se* objectionable: *Redwood Master Fund Ltd v. TD Bank Europe Ltd,
The Times*, January 30, 2003 (a decision relating to a syndicated loan agreement).
Similarly, if the decision, etc., results in an incidental benefit to one or more of
the other partners: see *Colin Gwyer & Associates Ltd v. London Wharf (Lime-
house) Ltd* [2003] 2 B.C.L.C. 153 at [76] (*per* Leslie Kosmin Q.C. sitting as a
deputy judge of the Chancery Division), concerning a decision by the directors
of a company. Where there is such an incidental benefit, the court is, however,
likely to scrutinise the circumstances with care: *ibid.* The position will be
otherwise where the decision is proved to be motivated by a collateral (and
improper) purpose: *ibid.* at [75], citing *Re Smith & Fawcett Ltd* [1942] Ch 304
at 306 (*per* Lord Greene M.R.) and *Howard Smith Ltd v. Ampol Petroleum Ltd*
[1974] A.C. 821; *Redwood Master Fund Ltd v. TD Bank Europe Ltd, supra.* In
Re Smith & Fawcett Ltd Lord Greene actually drew the analogy between private
companies and partnerships.

NOTE 27. See also *Deacons v. White & Case LLP, supra.*

The duty of honesty

Note, as to what may amount to "dishonesty" in this context, *Twinsectra Ltd v.*   **16–10**
Yardley, supra.

2. THE OBLIGATION OF PARTNERS NOT TO BENEFIT THEMSELVES AT THE EXPENSE OF THEIR CO-PARTNERS

Accountability of partners for private profits

16–12 In *John Taylors v. Masons* [2001] EWCA Civ 2106 (Lawtel 26/11/01), at [38], Arden L.J. observed that is a potential overlap between ss.29 and 42 of the Partnership Act 1890.

Needless to say the application of s.29 cannot be avoided by sheltering the benefit in a company or other third party. See *Lindsley v. Woodfull* [2004] 2 B.C.L.C. 131, CA, at [27] (*per* Arden L.J.); also *Trustor AB v. Smallbone (No.2)* [2001] 1 W.L.R. 1177; *CMS Dolphin Ltd v. Simonet* [2001] 2 B.C.L.C. 704.

Sale by or to the firm

Full disclosure

16–15 NOTE 50. And see also *Gwembe Valley Development Co Ltd v. Koshy* [2004] 1 B.C.L.C. 131, CA; *Murad v. Al-Saraj* [2005] EWCA Civ 959 (Lawtel 29/7/05).

Leases: renewal

Open renewal

16–21 Note also *John Taylors v. Masons, supra* and noticed *infra*, para.16–27, concerning open renewal of a *licence*.

Use of partnership property

Post-dissolution profits

16–27 The decision in *John Taylors v. Masons, supra*, is another example of a case in this class. There two of five partners brought about a dissolution of the firm on the precise date on which its licence from the District Council to conduct a market at certain premises expired. Prior to the date of dissolution, those partners obtained the grant of a provisional licence to run the market in place of the firm and some months later, pursuant to an open tender process, acquired a new 3-year licence. The Court of Appeal held that the opportunity to renew the licence was a partnership asset and that, in obtaining both the provisional and 3-year licences, the two partners had made use of the firm's business connection with the District Council. Accordingly, they were liable to account for the benefit of the goodwill which they had appropriated to themselves by engineering the grant of the new licences in their own favour and for any resulting profits. Arden L.J. also held that an overlapping claim might also be maintainable under the Partnership Act 1890, s.42: see *supra*, para.16–12.

See also *Lindsley v. Woodfull* [2004] 2 B.C.L.C. 131, CA, where an outgoing partner's continuing liability to account for profits under a contract (including all renewals thereof) was held to have been terminated as to the future by affirmation of a retirement agreement by the continuing partners. The outgoing partner was nevertheless held to be accountable for the value of the contract, including the prospective right of renewal, as at the date of his retirement.

NOTE 76. Note, in this connection, *Lindsley v. Woodfull, supra.*

Information gained as a partner

NOTE 80. Note also *Re Bhullar Bros Ltd* [2003] B.C.L.C. 241, CA.   **16–29**

CHAPTER 18

PARTNERSHIP PROPERTY

1. Partnership Property

18–06 In appropriate circumstances, the partnership property may comprise the shares in a company which, in commercial terms at least, carries on part (or even the whole) of the partnership business: see *National Westminster Bank plc v. Jones* [2001] 1 B.C.L.C. 98; *Dyment v. Boyden* [2004] B.C.L.C. 423, at [5]; *Chahal v. Mahal*, September 30, 2004 (Lawtel 5/10/04), and, on appeal, at [2005] EWCA Civ 898 (Lawtel 18/7/05). In the latter case, the *entire* partnership business had been transferred to and thereafter operated by the company.

Property paid for by the firm

18–07 *Bathurst v. Scarborow* [2005] 1 P. & C.R. 58, CA, is an example of such a case, despite the fact that the partners had agreed to purchase the land in question as joint tenants: see *infra*, para.19–15. See also *Mehra v. Shah,* August 1, 2003 (Lawtel 5/8/03) at [68], affirmed on appeal at [2004] EWCA Civ 632 (Lawtel 20/5/04).

In *Hardie's Executors v. Wales,* 2003 G.W.D. 13–448, OH, it was held that three insurance policies taken out on the life of a partner and paid for by the firm were partnership property. A similar result was achieved in the case of the second policy subject to the counterclaim in *Strover v. Strover, The Times*, May 30, 2005. The position would have been otherwise if the premiums had been treated as a drawing by the partner in question, even if the other partners were not aware of this: see *Pratt v. Medwin* [2003] EWCA Civ 906 (Lawtel 18/6/2003), at [13]; *Strover v. Strover, supra* (the first policy in issue).

Secret and other benefits obtained by a partner

18–15 NOTE 41. See further, as to the decisions in *Lister & Co v. Stubbs* and *Att.-Gen. for Hong Kong v. Reid, Daraydan Holdings Ltd v. Solland International Ltd* [2005] Ch. 119.

Property acquired after dissolution

18–17 In *John Taylors v. Masons* [2001] EWCA Civ 2106, two partners had brought about the dissolution of their firm with a view to securing the grant of a *new* licence to occupy the existing partnership premises in connection with their proposed business as livestock auctioneers. They first obtained a provisional licence, then a full three-year licence following an open tender process in which the other former partners participated. Despite this, they were held accountable to the dissolved firm, *inter alia*, for the value of the goodwill which existed in the opportunity to secure the new licences.

Intangible assets

Goodwill

The firm name may be an asset along with its associated goodwill, as in the case **18–19** of the "heavy metal" band Saxon: *Byford v. Oliver* [2003] E.M.L.R. 20.

Milk quota

NOTE 63. A note of the appeal in *Swift v. Dairywise Farms Ltd* now appears at **18–22** [2003] 1 W.L.R. 1606.

2. SEPARATE PROPERTY

Property used for partnership purposes

NOTE 88. See also *Latchman v. Pickard* [2005] EWHC 1011 (Ch) (Lawtel **18–33** 12/5/05).

Land

See also *Latchman v. Pickard, supra.* **18–35**

Outlays and improvements

NOTE 7. A note of the appeal in *Swift v. Dairywise Farms Ltd* now appears at **18–40** [2003] 1 W.L.R. 1606.

Proprietary estoppel

Note also *Strover v. Strover, The Times,* May 30, 2005, considered *infra,* **18–43** para.18–62.

NOTE 10. It has now been held that there may, in some cases, be no real difference between a constructive trust and a proprietary estoppel: *Oxley v. Hiscock* [2005] Q.B. 211. The reference to *Snells' Equity* should now be to the 31st ed. at paras 10–15 *et seq.*

3. ASSETS TRANSFERRED INTO OR OUT OF PARTNERSHIP

Note that such an agreement is now, seemingly, likely to attract a charge to stamp **18–45** duty land tax: see *infra*, para.38–21.

Agreements where intention unclear

18–58 Note 52. And see *Mehra v. Shah,* August 1, 2003 (Lawtel 5/8/03), affirmed on appeal at [2004] EWCA Civ 632 (Lawtel 20/5/04). There the fact that the Barking Road property was *omitted* from the firm's accounts was clearly not material.

Milk quota

18–61 Note 64. A note of the appeal in *Swift v. Dairywise Farms Ltd* now appears at [2003] 1 W.L.R. 1606.

Estoppel

18–62 A recent example of such a case is to be found in *Strover v. Strover, The Times* May 30, 2005, where an outgoing partner had, after his retirement, undertaken responsibility for payment of the premiums on a life insurance policy originally taken out for the benefit of the surviving partners in the event of his death. In holding that a proprietary estoppel arose in favour of the outgoing partner's estate, Hart J. held that this would affect entitlement to only 80 per cent of the policy monies, reflecting the relatively small probability that, if they had addressed the issue, the partners might have proceeded differently.

4. Legal Title to Partnership Property

Land

18–63 In an appropriate case, the partners may hold the land as joint tenants, both legally *and* beneficially: *Bathurst v. Scarborow* [2005] 1 P. & C.R. 58, CA. See *infra*, para.19–15.

Orders in relation to trusts of land

18–64 Note 74. For a consideration of manner in which the parties' intentions and purposes under *ibid.* s.15(1)(a) and (b) can affect the position and whether they can change over time, see *W v. W* [2004] 2 F.L.R. 321, CA.

Devolution of title

18–65 Note, as regards the beneficial interest, the decision in *Bathurst v. Scarborow* [2005] 1 P. & C.R. 58, *supra*, para.18–63.

CHAPTER 19

PARTNERSHIP SHARES

1. NATURE OF A PARTNERSHIP SHARE

Proprietary nature of a share

The internal and external perspectives

The application of the external perspective *may* become of relevance in certain **19–03** circumstances, *e.g.* when determining the manner in which a partnership share should be transferred: see *infra*, para.19–74. It might also conceivably be of relevance where a firm holds shares subject to a right of pre-emption, if one partner were to assign his partnership share: see the (ultimately inconclusive) discussion of the position of nominee shareholdings in *Rose v. Lynx Express Ltd* [2004] 1 B.C.L.C. 455.

The classic definition

In *Green v. Moran,* 2002 S.L.T. 1404, OH, an outgoing partner's action to **19–06** recover a fixed sum representing his perceived value of his share on retirement without taking an account was dismissed, *inter alia* on the basis that he had sought to "cherry pick" certain assets and ignored the firm's liabilities.

See also, as to the nature of a partner's interest in the partnership assets, *Byford v. Oliver* [2003] E.M.L.R. 20, at [19]; *Taylor v. Grier (No.3)*, May 12, 2003 (Lawtel 20/5/2003); *cf. Sandhu v Gill* [2005] 1 W.L.R. 1979, at [18].

The nature of a share—an analysis

(1) *Continuing partnership*

The majority of this passage was cited and applied by Evans-Lombe J. in **19–09** *Fengate Developments v. Customs & Excise Commissioners* [2004] S.T.C. 772, 776 at [14], [15]

(3) *Death, retirement or expulsion of a partner*

The second sentence was cited with apparent approval by Kevin Garnett Q.C. **19–12** sitting as a deputy judge of the Chancery Division in *Summers v. Smith*, March 27, 2002 (Lawtel 2/4/2002), at [64].

19–13 NOTE 46. See also *Green v. Moran*, 2002 S.L.T. 1404, OH.

The doctrine of non-survivorship between partners

19–15 It has now been held that, in an appropriate case, partners *may* agree to hold partnership property as joint tenants and that agreement will be respected by the courts: see *Bathurst v. Scarborow* [2005] 1 P. & C.R. 58, CA. In such cases the doctrine on non-survivorship will be displaced. As was pointed out by Rix L.J. at [52], this may be easier to demonstrate in the case of a partnership between husband and wife or the like.

5. THE TRANSFER OF A SHARE

Transfer allowed by agreement

19–68 The fact that such a transfer is permitted does not mean that the fundamental conditions for the existence of a partnership set out in the Partnership Act 1890, s.1(1) (see para.2–01) do not require to be satisfied as between the incoming partner and the continuing partners: *Backman v. R*, 3 I.T.L. Rep. 647, at [40]–[43] (Sup Ct (Can)).

Form of transfer

19–74 The views expressed in this paragraph represent what might be styled the orthodox approach, and are clearly supported by the decision of Kekewich J. in *Gray v. Smith* (1889) 43 Ch. D. 208, 212, to the effect that an agreement by a partner to retire and assign his share to the continuing partners would have to comply with the Statute of Frauds if the partnership assets comprise land (this issue was not, in the event, argued on appeal). See also *Ashworth v. Munn* (1878) 15 Ch. D. 367, albeit a decision under the Mortmain Act. However, the fact remains that, otherwise than under the external perspective (see para.19–03), a partner cannot properly be said to have a direct interest in any of the partnership assets, whatever their nature: see paras 19–06 *et seq.* The position in the case of co-owners is, inevitably, very different: see *Cooper v. Critchley* [1955] Ch. 431. It would seem a very odd result that the enforceability or otherwise of a contract for the transfer of a partnership share ultimately depends on whether the partnership assets consist of land at a given point in time, *e.g.* where land is acquired after the contract is concluded or where it is disposed of between contract and completion. Perhaps the ultimate rationale is that the court will have regard only to the external perspective and will not concern itself with the internal financial arrangements between the partners; *sed quaere*.

Be that as it may, there is no doubt that the doctrine of constructive trusts remains unaffected by the statutory provisions quoted in the text: see the Law of Property Act 1925, s.53(2) and the Law of Property (Miscellaneous Provisions) Act 1989, s.2(5). Thus, if the assignment were effected verbally and the assignee were then admitted to the partnership and treated as entitled to the assignor's share, it is difficult to see why a constructive trust should not arise in the former's favour.

The application of stamp duty land tax to various partnership transactions by the Finance Acts 2003 and 2004 has, of course, reduced the importance of the issues canvassed above, since the existence or otherwise of a document evidencing an assignment is no longer determinative of whether a charge to tax can be imposed. See further, *infra*, paras 38–16 *et seq.*

Note 35. The definition now reads merely "'interest in land' means any estate, interest or charge in or over land": see the Trusts of Land and Appointment of Trustees Act 1996, Sch.4.

CHAPTER 20

THE FINANCIAL RIGHTS AND DUTIES OF A PARTNER

1. DEBTS, LIABILITIES AND LOSSES

Repudiation of partnership

20–17 It is now clear that the doctrine of repudiation does not apply: see *infra*, paras 24–05, 24–06.

Civil Liability (Contribution) Act 1978

20–21 See also, as to the meaning of "the same damage", *Royal Brompton Hospital NHS Trust v. Hammond* [2002] 1 W.L.R. 1397, HL; *Hurstwood Developments Ltd v. Motor & General & Aldersley & Co Insurance Services Ltd* [2002] P.N.L.R. 10, CA.

4. REMUNERATION FOR SERVICES RENDERED TO FIRM

Exceptions to the general rule

Services rendered after dissolution

20–48 In *Emerson v. Estate of Emerson* [2004] 1 B.C.L.C. 575, CA, the surviving partner was held to be entitled to an allowance, even though the business had been making trading losses. The quantum of the allowance ultimately equalled the losses he had incurred.

CHAPTER 21

ASCERTAINMENT AND DIVISION OF PROFITS

Method of accounting

The proposition advanced in the text can no longer be regarded as valid. In **21–04**
November 2003 the Accounting Standards Board issued Application Note G,
entitled "Revenue Recognition", to Financial Reporting Standard 5 ("Reporting
the Substance of Transactions"), under which all firms engaged in the supply of
goods and services are, in general, required to produce accounts which recognise
income as and when they can properly be regarded as entitled thereto, even in the
case of a contract which is ongoing. Only where the right to consideration can
truly be said not to have arisen, *e.g.* in the case of a fee payable only on a
contingency, will it be possible to ignore this principle. Although strong representations were made against the introduction of this approach as regards contracts for services, on March 10, 2005 the Urgent Issues Taskforce issued
Abstract 40 ("Revenue recognition and service contracts"), confirming its application and giving further guidance in the case of firms working under such
contracts. The UITF also confirmed that accounts complying with this requirement should be produced in respect of any accounting period ending on or after
June 22, 2005: see *ibid.* para.30.

It should also be noted that the Income Tax (Trading and Other Income) Act
2005, s.25(1) requires accounts to be prepared "in accordance with generally
accepted accounting practice", rather than on an "accounting basis which gives
a true and fair view" (*i.e.* the former wording in the Finance Act 1998, s.42(1),
prior to the amendment effected by the Finance Act 2002, s.103(5)). It necessarily follows that Application Note G must be taken into account when computing the firm's profits for tax purposes.

Time and manner of division

NOTE 22. Note that the division of profits (as opposed to the manner in which **21–07**
they are to be *shared* between the partners) is ultimately a matter of internal
management: *Stevens v. South Devon Railway Co* (1851) 9 Hare 313, 326, *per* Sir
G.J. Turner V.-C.; see also *Burland v. Earle* [1902] A.C. 83, 95.

CHAPTER 22

PARTNERSHIP ACCOUNTS

1. The Manner in which Accounts should be Kept

Other funds held by the firm

22–04 Note 7. See now the Income Tax (Trading and Other Income) Act 2005, s.25(1). This may include work in progress brought into account as a result of the recent changes to FRS5: see *supra*, para.21–04.

Annual accounts

22–07 The Income Tax (Trading and Other Income) Act 2005, s.25(1) requires accounts to be prepared "in accordance with generally accepted accounting practice", rather than on a "true and fair" basis as before (see the Finance Act 1998, s.42(1) prior to the amendment introduced by the Finance Act 2002, s.103(5)). This will (*inter alia*) entail compliance with the requirements of Application Note G (entitled "Revenue Recognition") to Financial Reporting Standard 5 ("Reporting the Substance of Transactions"), issued by the Accounting Standards Board in November 2003, which requires firms to recognise income in their accounts as and when a right to it arises. See further, *supra*, para.21–04.

22–08 *Corporate partnerships:* It should be noted that, whilst the Partnerships and Unlimited Companies (Accounts) Regulations 1993 require the like annual accounts as "would be required under Part VII" of the Companies Act 1985 (*ibid.* reg.4(1)), not all the UK GAAP requirements need to be complied with: see *ibid.* reg.4(3), Sch. (as prospectively amended by the Partnerships and Unlimited Companies (Accounts) (Amendment) Regulations 2005 (SI 2005/1987), reg.3), modifying the application of the 1985 Act. The Regulations do not apply the other provisions of the 1985 Act, *e.g.* the prohibition on distributions contained in *ibid.* s.263.

As to the application of the Regulations to limited partnerships, see further, *infra,* para.31–25.

Note 20. *Ibid.* Sched. is prospectively amended by the Partnerships and Unlimited Companies (Accounts) (Amendment) Regulations 2005, reg.3.

Note 24. *Ibid.* reg.7 is prospectively amended by the Partnerships and Unlimited Companies (Accounts) (Amendment) Regulations 2005, reg.2.

2. THE PARTNERS' RIGHTS AND OBLIGATIONS

The primary duty

The right of access afforded to each partner under s.24(9) of the Partnership Act **22–10** 1890 provided the foundation for the decision in *Wan v. General Commissioners for Division of Doncaster*, 76 T.C. 211. There a penalty was held to have been properly imposed on each partner for failure to provide information to the Inspector of Taxes which any of them could have obtained by exercising that right.

CHAPTER 23

ACTIONS BETWEEN PARTNERS

3. Cases in which the Court will not Interfere Between Partners

Rule 3: The court will not interfere at the instance of a partner guilty of laches or acquiescence

23–18   Note 63. See also *Patel v. Shah*, *The Times*, March 2, 2005.

Agreements for partnership and laches/acquiescence

23–20   This passage was approved and applied in *Patel v. Shah*, *supra*.

Evidence of abandonment, etc.

23–24   Note 77. See also *Patel v. Shah*, *supra*.

4. Limitation as between Partners

Dissolved partnership

23–34   This analysis was approved by Lightman J. in *Sandhu v Gill* [2005] 1 W.L.R. 1979, at [12].

Note 20. See also *Mehra v. Shah*, August 1, 2003 (Lawtel 5/8/03), at [74] (*per* Sonia Proudman Q.C. sitting as a deputy judge of the Chancery Division). This aspect was not pursued on the appeal at [2004] EWCA Civ 632 (Lawtel 20/5/04).

NOTE 24. Note that, in *Harper v. John C. Harper & Co*, 2003 S.L.T. 102, Sh Ct, **23–35** it appears to have been held that the right to an account did not arise under the agreement, so that the general law applied for limitation purposes under Scots law. *Quaere*, could a similar argument be raised under *ibid*. s.8(1)?

Right to an account

Acknowledgment

NOTE 30. Note that, in *Harper v. John C. Harper & Co*, *supra*, a partner had **23–37** acknowledged a former partner's right to an account in his personal capacity and this was held also to be binding in his capacity as a partner. The two partners in question were former spouses.

Trusts and fiduciary relationships

NOTE 50. See also *Gwembe Valley Development Co Ltd v. Koshy (No.3)* [2004] **23–43** 1 B.C.L.C. 131, CA. *Cf*. the decision in *Patel v. Shah, supra*.

5. ACTIONS FOR SPECIFIC PERFORMANCE

Agreements for partnership: the general rule

NOTE 60. Note also *Lauritzencool AB v. Lady Navigation Inc*, *The Times*, May 26, **23–45** 2005, CA, which concerned the grant of negative injunctive relief.

6. ACTIONS FOR FRAUD AND MISREPRESENTATION

B. RESCISSION

Agreements for partnership

NOTES 85, 86, 87. See now *Chitty on Contracts* (29th ed.), paras 6–096, 6–097 **23–53** and 6–100 respectively.

Loss of right to rescind

Laches, acquiescence and affirmation

In *Lindsley v. Woodfull* [2004] 2 B.C.L.C. 131, CA, two partners affirmed the **23–66** retirement of a third at a time when they were aware of his previous mis-representation, and thereby lost their right to an account of *future* profits resulting from his breaches of fiduciary duty prior to his retirement. Their right to an account of past profits had been expressly reserved.

Reconstituting a partnership by rescission

23–68   An attempt to reconstitute a joint venture agreement by rescission failed in *Huyton SA v. Distribuidora Internacional de Productos Agricolas SA* [2004] 1 All E.R. (Comm) 402, CA, at [5]. Note, however, that in *Roberts v. West Coast Trains Ltd* [2004] I.R.L.R. 788, CA, it was held that an employment contract could be reconstituted following a dismissal, albeit pursuant to an internal appeals procedure.

7. RELIEF COMMONLY SOUGHT BETWEEN PARTNERS

A. ACCOUNTS, INQUIRIES AND PRODUCTION OF DOCUMENTS

(a) The right to an account, inquiries and production of documents

(1) *Accounts and inquiries*

Account normally required between partners

23–75   See also, as to the general rule, *Green v. Moran*, 2002 S.L.T. 1404, OH, noticed *supra*, para.19–06. However, the general rule was held not to be applicable where the financial position between the partners had been determined by an arbitration award which was then remitted to the arbitrator for amendment. Since the award continued to have legal effect, the need for an account was not resurrected: see *Carter v. Harold Simpson Associates (Architects) Ltd* [2005] 1 W.L.R. 919, PC.

   Note than an account may not be an appropriate remedy in the case of a breach of a restraint covenant by a *former* partner: see *WWF-World Wide Fund for Nature v. World Wresting Federation Entertainment Inc* [2002] F.S.R. 504; *cf. Experience Hendrix LLC v. PPX Enterprises Inc* [2003] 1 All E.R. (Comm) 830, at [32]. See also *supra*, para.10–234A.

Interim orders: payment into court

Payment in pending trial

23–91   NOTE 35. See, generally, as to the circumstances in which a payment in may be ordered under the CPR, r.25.1(1), *Myers v. Design Inc (International) Ltd* [2003] 1 W.L.R. 1642.

(2) *Production of documents, etc.*

Right to production of documents

23–96   Partners are now supplementing their traditional rights to production of documents by making data subject access applications under the Data Protection Act 1998, s.7. Whether this actually adds anything useful, other than a further tier of complexity is, in the current editor's view, doubtful: note, in this connection, *Johnson v. Medical Defence Union Ltd* [2005] 1 W.L.R. 750.

(b) Defences to an action for an account

(ii) *Settled account*

Nature of settled account

NOTE 12. Note also *Pelosi v. Luca*, July 8, 2004, OH, at [21].　　**23–109**

(iv) *Accord and satisfaction*

NOTES 40, 41. See now *Chitty on Contracts* (29th ed.), paras 22–012 *et seq.*, **23–116**
22–015 respectively.

(vi) *Release*

NOTE 44. See now *Chitty on Contracts* (29th ed.), paras 22–003 *et seq.*　　**23–118**

NOTE 47. See now *Chitty on Contracts* (29th ed.), para.22–003.

(c) Judgments for partnership account

Form of judgment

NOTE 54. As to what is required where the order also directs all vouching **23–119**
documents to be produced, see *Sahota v. Sohi* [2004] EWHC 1469 (Ch) (Lawtel
8/7/04).

Costs

Solicitor's lien and charge for costs

NOTE 72. Note also, as to waiver of this lien, *Clifford Harris & Co v. Solland* **23–123**
International Ltd (No.2) [2005] 2 All E.R. 334.

Taking the account

Just allowances

In *Emerson v. Estate of Emerson* [2004] 1 B.C.L.C. 575, CA, an allowance was **23–126**
made in the amount of a loss incurred by the surviving partner in carrying on the
business following the death of his partner.

Evidence on which accounts are taken

For a recent example of a case where clients' files had been improperly removed **23–129**
from the partnership premises and subsequently lost and the resulting presump-
tions made against the accounting party, see *Finlayson v. Turnbull (No.4)*, 2003
G.W.D. 12–374, OH. Note also that the mere fact that certain figures produced by
each side are similar may not be determinative: *Gharavi-Nakhjavani v. Pelagias*,
June 17, 2005 (Lawtel 20/6/05), CA.

B. INJUNCTIONS

Injunction without a dissolution

Exclusion

23–137 NOTE 37. As to payment of an occupation rent, see also *Abbott v. Price* [2003] EWHC 2760 (Ch) at [112] *et seq.* (Lawtel 26/11/03); *Re Byford* [2004] 1 F.L.R. 56.

Attempts to frustrate the decision making process

23–142 NOTE 50. There are, of course, no such powers as exist under the Companies Act 1985, s.371 in the case of a partnership: *Cf. Re Woven Rugs Ltd* [2002] 1 B.C.L.C. 324.

Injunction in dissolution actions

23–145 *Assets:* Equally, in *Latchman v. Pickard* [2005] EWHC 1011 (Ch) (Lawtel 12/5/05), an interim injunction permitting one partner to have access to the former partnership premises was refused, ultimately because of the practical difficulties which this was likely to cause: *ibid.* at [25]. Warren J. expressed a strong preference for the appointment of a receiver in all the circumstances, although no application for such an appointment was before him.

C. RECEIVERS

Purpose and desirability of appointing a receiver and manager

23–153 NOTE 99. See now CPR, Pt 69 and 69PD.

Nature of partnership business

23–154 See *Latchman v. Pickard, supra*, where Warren J. expressed certain views (albeit on an *obiter* basis) as to the desirability of appointing a receiver in relation to a medical partnership.

Identity and remuneration of receiver

23–175 See now CPR, r.69.3, 69PD, paras 4.2 *et seq.*

Remuneration etc.

23–177 See now CPR, r.69.7, 69PD, para.9.

Powers of receiver

23–179 Note that a receiver may apply to the court for directions: see CPR, r.69.6 and 69PD, para.8.

Liability of receiver

Semble, a receiver will not be personally liable for tax in respect of his realisa- **23–180** tions of partnership property, etc.: *Re Piacentini* [2003] Q.B. 1497 (a decision concerning a receiver appointed under the Criminal Justice Act, s.77).

Where it is alleged that the receiver has mismanaged the business, the only recoverable loss is that suffered by the partners *as such*: see *McGowan v. Chadwick* [2003] B.P.I.R. 647, CA.

D. ORDERS FOR THE SALE OF PARTNERSHIP PROPERTY

Agreements excluding the normal rule

NOTE 20. *Green v. Moran*, 2002 S.L.T. 1404, OH, was another example of such **23–184** a case, albeit that a sale of assets was not sought.

The court's discretion

See also, as to the feasibility of selling a professional insolvency practice, **23–186** *Mullins v. Laughton* [2003] Ch. 250, at [118], *per* Neuberger J.

Syers v. Syers orders

Hoffmann's L.J.'s views were cited by Neuberger J. in *Mullins v. Laughton*, **23–188** *supra*, at [110].

As regards proposition (d), Neuberger J. was prepared to make a mandatory order **23–189** in *Mullins v. Laughton*, *supra*, at [112]. Equally, he threatened to revisit the question of an order for sale if the valuation process consequent on the proposed *Syers v. Syers* order was unnecessarily drawn out: see *ibid.* at [134].

As regards proposition (g), in *Mullins v. Laughton*, *supra*, at [123], Neuberger J. **23–190** regarded it as conceivable that the partner bought out might end up as a net debtor to the partnership. *Quaere* should the court's discretion be exercised in such a case. It was also accepted, based on a concession by the defendants, that certain indemnities against partnership liability were appropriate: *ibid.* at [132].

Despite what is stated in proposition (h), *Mullins v. Laughton*, *supra*, was a case in which an order was made that the defendants buy out the claimant, *despite* their misconduct, in order to do justice between the parties: *ibid.* at [112] *et seq.*

Proposition (i) was cited by Neuberger J. with apparent approval in *Mullins v. Laughton*, *supra*, at [111].

NOTE 47. *Profinance Trust SA v. Gladstone* is now reported at [2002] 1 B.C.L.C. 141: see especially at *ibid.* p.160; also *Re Clearsprings (Management) Ltd* [2003] EWHC 2516 (Ch) (Lawtel 21/11/03), at [32], [33].

Unsaleable but valuable assets

23–198 *National Health Service goodwill:* The argument canvassed in the text as to the permissible options regarding patients no longer holds good in the face of the revocation of the National Health Service (General Medical Services) Regulations 1992 by the General Medical Services and Personal Medical Services Transitional and Consequential Provisions Order 2004 (SI 2004/865). Under the National Health Service (General Medical Services Contracts) Regulations 2004 (SI 2004/291), a general medical services contract will be entered into between a Primary Care Trust (PCT) and the *partnership*, as opposed to each individual doctor (see *ibid.* reg.11) and, consistently therewith, the partnership will have its own list of patients (*ibid.* Sch.6, Pt 2, paras 14, 15). Such a contract will subsist until it is terminated in accordance with its terms or the general law (*ibid.* reg.14(1)) and should contain arrangements applicable on such termination (*ibid.* reg.25). It would seem that a dissolution will not necessarily bring about a termination, although much will depend on the terms of the contract: see *Latchman v. Pickard* [2005] EWHC 1011 (Ch) (Lawtel 12/5/05), at [2]. It is possible for the contract to be continued with *one* of the former partners pursuant to the variation procedure under *ibid.* Sch.6, Pt 8, para.106(1). The notice nominating the former partner must be signed by all the partners (*ibid.* para. 106(3)(c)), so that competing notices would seem to be an impossibility. The Regulations do not lay down a procedure under which a *group* of former partners can apply to continue the contract. In such a case, each group can apply for the new contract and it will be for the PCT to decide how to deal with the matter: see *Latchman v. Pickard, supra,* at [3]. The PCT may permit only one new contract: *ibid.* In the case of a two partner firm, on the death of one partner the contract will continue with the surviving partner if he is suitably qualified: *ibid.* para.106(4), (4A), as amended/added by the National Health Service (Primary Medical Services) (Miscellaneous Amendments) Regulations 2005 (SI 2005/893), reg.4(20).

NOTE 87. The National Health Service Act 1977, s.54 has been further amended by the Health and Social Care (Community Health and Standards) Act 2003, Sch.11, para.26 and *ibid.* Sch.10 has been further amended by *ibid.* Sch.11, para.43. A further prohibition on the sale of goodwill by various types of contractors and certain medical practitioners providing "essential services" is also to be found in the Primary Medical Services (Sale of Goodwill and Restrictions on Sub-contracting) Regulations 2004 (SI 2004/906), reg.3(1).

Other potentially anomalous assets

23–199 *Work in progress:* Note also *Champion v. Workman*, June 20, 2001 (Lawtel 22/8/01), noticed *supra*, para.23–159; *Finlayson v. Turnbull (No.4)*, 2003 G.W.D. 12–374, OH. Equally, account must also now be taken of the manner in which partnership accounts are required to be drawn up: see *supra*, para.21–04.

Milk quota

23–201 NOTE 6. A note of the appeal in *Swift v. Dairywise Farms Ltd* now appears at [2003] 1 W.L.R. 1606.

Interim order for sale

As to the circumstances in which a court will order a sale of assets on an interim **23–203** basis (albeit under the pre-CPR regime), see On *Demand Information PLC v. Michael Grierson (Finance) PLC* [2003] 1 A.C. 368, HL.

8. ACTIONS FOR DAMAGES

The right to damages as between partners

The modern law

Note that, in *Mullins v. Laughton* [2003] Ch. 250, Neuberger J. accepted the **23–208** principle that an action for damages for loss of reputation would lie as between partners: see *ibid.* at [128] to [131].

NOTE 43. See now, as to the applicability of the doctrine of repudiation, *infra*, paras 24–05, 24–06.

Part Five

DISSOLUTION AND WINDING-UP

CHAPTER 24

DISSOLUTION AND ITS CAUSES

1. INTRODUCTION

Meaning of dissolution

Distinction between technical and general dissolution

The distinction between a technical and general dissolution was accepted in **24–03** *Summers v. Smith*, March 27, 2002 (Lawtel 27/3/02) at para.[65].

The doctrine of repudiation

Hurst v. Bryk is now reported at [2002] 1 A.C. 185. In *Mullins v. Laughton* [2003] **24–05,** Ch. 250, Neuberger J. adopted the *obiter* views voiced by Lord Millett in *Hurst* **24–06** *v. Bryk* and held that the doctrine of repudiation had no application to partnerships, albeit only after brief oral argument: see *ibid.* at [93]. It should be noted that, in reaching his conclusion, Neuberger J. contrasted the views expressed by the current editor in para.24–06 of this work with those set out in para.6.29 of the Law Commission's Consultation Paper No.159 (2000) on Partnership Law: see *ibid.* at [91]. Unknown to his Lordship, much of the reasoning set out in that paragraph of the Consultation Paper was derived from an earlier draft of Chapter 24 of this work, representing the current editor's preliminary views whilst absorbing the full implications of Lord Millett's speech. Neuberger J.'s conclusion that an accepted repudiation could not dispense with the agreement but leave the partnership relationship in place is clearly right.

Extraordinarily, despite the above decisions, repudiation arguments are still, in practice, continuing to be advanced.

24–07 The views expressed in this paragraph did not find favour with Neuberger J. in *Mullins v. Laughton, supra*, at [92], albeit allowing that they do not represent "a negligible point".

Agreements to which the doctrine can still apply

24–07A It should be noted that the objections to the application of the doctrine voiced in *Hurst v. Bryk* and *Mullins v. Laughton* do not apply in the case of an agreement between partners which does not regulate their relationship as partners, as noted in para.24–06. Thus, an agreement regulating the terms of a partner's *retirement* could be repudiated, as could a dissolution agreement. In *Jenkins v. Holy* (Lawtel 25/6/04), a repudiation argument relating to a retirement agreement did not succeed but, as currently reported, it is not clear on what basis. There can be little doubt that an LLP members' agreement can be the subject of a repudiation since, unlike a partnership, its continued application is not inextricably bound up with the continued existence of the LLP.

Albeit in some respects similar to a partnership (see para.5–07), a joint venture agreement can clearly be repudiated: *Dymocks Franchise Systems (NSW) Pty Ltd v. Todd* [2002] 2 All E.R. (Comm) 849 (PC).

Nature of the breach etc.

24–08 to These paragraphs are now of limited relevance, whilst the decision in *Mullins v.*
24–11 *Laughton, supra,* stands. It should, nevertheless, be noted that, subject only to his conclusion on the inapplicability of the doctrine, Neuberger J. would have found the conduct of the defendants sufficient to amount to a repudiation: see *ibid.* at [94] *et seq.*

The doctrine of frustration

24–12 As from a day to be appointed, the Mental Health Act 1983, s.96(1)(g) will be repealed by the Mental Capacity Act 2005, Sch.7. The powers of the Court thereunder appear to be less extensive than under the 1983 Act: see *infra*, para.24–47.

2. DISSOLUTION OTHERWISE THAN BY THE COURT

A. EXPIRATION OF TERM, ETC.

Continuation after fixed term: the statutory presumptions

24–15 NOTE 85. For another example of a case in which partners were treated as having adopted a draft agreement, albeit otherwise than following the expiration of a fixed term, see *Thakrar v. Vadera*, March 31, 1999 (unreported).

B. NOTICE

When notice will dissolve

Fraud and mala fides

The ability to set aside a dissolution notice given in bad faith was conceded in **24–20**
Thakrar v. Vadera, March 31, 1999 (unreported).

Dissolution inferred although no notice

The proposition in the text holds good notwithstanding the views expressed in **24–25**
Hurst v. Bryk [2002] 1 A.C. 185 and *Mullins v. Laughton* [2003] Ch. 250, which
were clearly not made in the context of a partnership at will. For a recent
affirmation of this, see *Chahal v. Mahal* [2005] EWCA Civ 898 (Lawtel 18/7/05),
where the Court of Appeal held that incorporation of a partnership business will
usually (but not invariably) result in a dissolution being inferred: see further
infra, para.24–45. Another example (albeit in the VAT and Duties Tribunal) is to
be found in *Hussein v. Commissioners of Customs & Excise* [2003] V. & D.R.
439, at [38].

E. ILLEGALITY

Illegality caused by one partner

Bower v. Hughes Hooker & Co, March 27, 2003, EAT, was a similar case to **24–44**
Hudgell Yeates & Co v. Watson, although the partner in question had been struck
off. The dissolution issue was not pursued on appeal: see *Stevens v. Bower* [2004]
I.R.L.R. 957. The bankruptcy of a partner in a firm of solicitors will have the
same effect, since it will result in his practising certificate being suspended. See
also, as to the effects of an intervention by the Law Society into such a firm, *Rose
v. Dodd*, *The Times*, August 16, 2005 (and Lawtel 27/7/05), CA (although the
views expressed there were strictly *obiter*).

F. CESSATION OF BUSINESS

The views expressed by Neuberger J. in *National Westminster Bank Plc v. Jones* **24–45**
were echoed in *Chahal v. Mahal*, September 30, 2004 (Lawtel 5/10/04), where
the entire partnership business had been transferred to a company. It was held that
this transfer did not bring about an automatic dissolution. Although this decision
was upheld on appeal at [2005] EWCA Civ 898 (Lawtel 18/7/05), the Court of
Appeal expressed the view that where a partnership business is incorporated and
shares are issued to the partners in proportion to their partnership interests, it will
usually be appropriate to infer that a dissolution has occurred: see *ibid.* at [17],
[29], [36]. The position is likely to be otherwise if the shares become partnership
property or if one partner has been kept in ignorance of the incorporation: *ibid.*
[36], [38], [39]. And note also *Dyment v. Boyden* [2004] B.C.L.C. 423, at [5].

3. DISSOLUTION BY THE COURT

A. STATUTES UNDER WHICH A PARTNERSHIP MAY BE DISSOLVED

Mental Health Act 1983, sections 95 and 96

24–47 As from a day to be appointed, these sections will be repealed by the Mental Capacity Act 2005. Where a partner lacks capacity (see *ibid.* s.2), it seems that the Court may only order a decision to be taken on his behalf "which will have the effect of dissolving a partnership of which [he] is a member: *ibid.* s.18(1)(e), read with s.16. This would clearly include service of a notice of dissolution under the agreement or under the Partnership Act 1890, s.26(1) and/or 32(c) but, unlike the position under the 1983 Act, there is seemingly no power for the court to order a dissolution, otherwise than in the usual way pursuant to s.35 of the 1890 Act.

NOTE 87. See also *Masterman Lister v. Jewell* [2003] 3 All E.R. 162, CA.

Insolvency Act 1986

24–48 Concurrent petitions against the partners may now also in certain circumstances accompany not only the presentation of a creditor's petition but also the presentation of a petition by a liquidator or a temporary administrator: Insolvent Partnerships Order 1994, art.8(1), as amended by the Insolvent Partnerships (Amendment) Order 2002 (SI 2002/1308), art.4. In such cases, a second ground for the petition has now been added, namely that, when a moratorium under the Insolvency Act 1986, s.1A ends, no voluntary arrangement approved under *ibid.* Pt 1 has effect: *ibid.* s.221(8)(b), as amended the Insolvent Partnerships Order 1994, Sch.4, Pt I, para.3, as itself amended by the Insolvent Partnerships (Amendment) (No.2) Order 2002 (SI 2002/2708), art.9(2). A identical ground has also been added in the case of a petition presented solely against the firm, provided that it is presented by one or more creditors: *ibid.* s.227(7)(d), (7A) as added by the Insolvent Partnerships Order 1994, Sch.3, para.3, as itself amended by the Insolvent Partnerships (Amendment) (No.2) Order 2002, art.8.

NOTE 93. The Insolvent Partnerships Order 1994, art.7(1) has been amended by the Insolvent Partnerships (Amendment) Order 2002, art.3.

Administration orders, etc.

24–49 The same rule will now apply whenever a partnership is in or seeking to enter administration, whether by means of the making of an administration order or the appointment of an administrator outside court: Insolvency Act 1986, Sch.B1, paras 42(1), (4), 44(1), (2), (5), as substituted and applied by the Insolvent Partnerships Order 1994, art.6(1), Sch.2, para.17, as (in the case of para.42) substituted by the Insolvent Partnerships (Amendment) Order 2005 (SI 2005/1516), art.7.

Moratorium under the Insolvency Act 1986, Sch.A1

Similarly, a court will not have jurisdiction to make an order under s.35 of the **24–49A**
1890 Act whilst a moratorium is in place to facilitate the proposal of a partnership voluntary arrangement: Insolvency Act 1986, Sch.A1, para.12(1)(j), as
substituted and applied by the Insolvent Partnerships Order 1994, art.4(1), Sch.1,
as respectively substituted by the Insolvent Partnerships (Amendment) (No.2)
Order 2002 (SI 2002/2708), arts 4, 6. See further *infra*, para.27–171A.

Firms providing financial services

NOTE 9. The Insolvent Partnerships Order 1994, art.19(4) has been further **24–50**
amended by the Insolvent Partnerships (Amendment) (No.2) Order 2002, art.5.

B. JURISDICTION TO DISSOLVE A PARTNERSHIP

Transfer of proceedings between High Court and county court

As to transfer to the county court, see (2004) L.S.G., October 14, p.37. See also, **24–53**
as to mental incapacity, *supra*, para.24–47.

Foreign court

NOTE 37. *Philips v. Symes* is now reported at [2002] 1 W.L.R. 853. **24–54**

D. GROUNDS FOR DISSOLUTION

Overriding discretion of court

See also *Mullins v. Laughton* [2003] Ch. 250 at [108], *per* Neuberger J. And see, **24–58**
as to the prospective repeal of Part VII of the Mental Health Act 1983, *supra*,
para.24–47.

(a) **Mental Disorder**

Effect of Mental Health Acts 1959 and 1983

Part VII of the Mental Health Act 1983 is due, as from a day to be appointed, to **24–60**
be repealed by the Mental Capacity Act 2005, Sch.7: see further, *supra*,
para.24–47.

NOTE 64. See also *Masterman Lister v. Jewell* [2003] 3 All E.R. 162, CA.

Exercise of discretion, etc.

See, *supra*, para.24–47. **24–61 to**
24–64

(d) Breach of the Agreement and Destruction of Mutual Confidence

Reluctance of court to interfere

24–78 NOTE 11. In *Thakrar v. Vadera*, March 31, 1999 (unreported) Arden J., when considering a power of expulsion exercisable in a case falling with this ground, observed that "trivial breaches would not lead the court to exercise its powers . . . ".

Nature and degree of misconduct

24–81 For a further example of the type of conduct required to invoke this ground, see *Mullins v. Laughton* [2003] Ch. 250, considered *supra*, paras 24–05 *et seq*. And note *Re Baumler (UK) Ltd* [2005] 1 B.C.L.C. 92, albeit a decision concerning a quasi-partnership company on an application under the Companies Act 1985, s.459; *cf. McKee v. O'Reilly* [2003] EWHC 2008 (Ch) (Lawtel 19/9/03), another s.459 case.

(f) The Just and Equitable Ground

24–86 An order on this ground was in fact made in *Thakrar v. Vadera*, March 31, 1999 (unreported) and in *Mullins v. Laughton* [2003] Ch. 250, considered *supra*, paras 24–05 *et seq*.

Quaere is there any scope under this ground for invoking the "last straw" test recognised in employment cases, such *Omilaju v Waltham Forest LBC* [2005] 1 All E.R. 75, CA.

Conduct of the applicant(s)

24–87 In *Thakrar v. Vadera*, March 31, 1999 (unreported), Arden J. expressly held that the conduct of the applicant does not exclude him from obtaining an order on this ground, but went on to observe that "the court would be loath to exercise the jurisdiction at the request of a party who is responsible for the breakdown of mutual trust and confidence."

E. Date of Dissolution

24–88 In *Mullins v. Laughton* [2003] Ch. 250, Neuberger J. recognised that the dissolution could only have effect as from the date of his judgment, but nevertheless allowed the claimant to elect as between that date and the date of his exclusion from the partnership for the purposes of taking certain accounts. The basis on which he did so is, however, open to doubt, even allowing for his expressed disapproval of the defendants' behaviour.

CHAPTER 25

WINDING UP THE PARTNERSHIP AFFAIRS

1. CONSEQUENCES OF DISSOLUTION

Employees

The proposition in this passage was considered by the Court of Appeal in *Rose* **25–02**
v. Dodd [2005] EWCA Civ 957 (Lawtel 27/7/05) at [49], in the context of
expressing *obiter* views as to the effect of an intervention in a solicitors' practice
(this does not appear from the report in *The Times*, August 16, 2005). The Court
appeared to accept that there may be cases where employment can continue
following a general dissolution, citing *inter alia* the potential application of s.38
of the Partnership Act 1890. Equally, if one or more of the members of the
dissolved firm continue to carry on the business following the dissolution and are
treated as having re-engaged the former firm's staff, they will in any event enjoy
continuity of employment by virtue of the Employment Rights Act 1996,
s.218(5): *Stevens v. Bower* [2004] I.R.L.R. 957, CA, applying *obiter* views
expressed in *Jeetle v. Elster* [1985] I.C.R. 389.

Transfer of Undertakings (Protection of Employment) Regulations 1981

This passage was also quoted by the Court of Appeal in *Rose v. Dodd, supra,* at **25–03**
[57]. The Court was clearly not prepared to lay down any hard and fast rules as
to whether TUPE would apply in a given case and emphasised that much would
depend on the particular circumstances: *ibid.* at [58]. The Regulations were
clearly regarded as applicable by the Employment Appeal Tribunal in *Hynd v.
Armstrong*, September 20, 2004 (Lawtel 20/10/04), where a Scottish firm of
solicitors was demerging to form two separate firms. Equally, the employee had
seemingly been dismissed *prior* to the demerger: see [5]. *Quaere*, will the
Regulations apply where a group of partners *de facto* take over part of the
goodwill of the firm on dissolution, *otherwise* than by means of a formal

purchase. It would seem that they might: see, for example, *Fairhurst Ward Abbotts Ltd v. Botes Building Ltd* [2004] I.C.R. 919, CA (albeit not a partnership case).

Note also that new TUPE Regulations are due to come into force in the near future, although what precise form they will take is not yet known.

Occupation of premises

25–04 Note that, in *Latchman v. Pickard* [2005] EWHC 1011 (Ch) (Lawtel 12/5/05), it seems to have been held that Dr. Latchman's implied licence over part of the partnership premises had been terminated, even though the firm's contract with the Primary Care Trust still had some time to run. Although she had a continuing licence to occupy the remainder of the premises, she was refused injunctive relief because of the state of her relationship with the other partners.

2. The Return of Premiums

C. Partnership for a Fixed Term

Cause of dissolution

(4) *Mental disorder*

25–17 It would seem that, when the Mental Health Act 1983, ss.95, 96 are repealed by the Mental Capacity Act 2005, Sch.7, a dissolution will only be achievable under the 1890 Act jurisdiction, so that the position will be as described in the remaining paragraphs under this heading. See also, *supra*, para.24–47.

3. The Treatment of Post Dissolution Profits

Partnership Act 1890, section 42

25–25 Note 80. See, as to the meaning of the expression "his share in the partnership assets", *Sandhu v. Gill* [2005] 1 W.L.R. 1979, at [18]. See further, *infra*, para.25–28.

Note 81. In its Report on Partnership Law of November 2003 (Law Com No.283), the Law Commission clearly recognised the need for a commercial rate of interest to be paid, albeit that retention of s.42 was not, in the event, advocated: see *ibid.*, paras 8–53, 8–74.

Nature of the option under section 42(1)

25–28 In *Sandhu v. Gill*, *supra*, Lightman J. held that, if a claimant seeks a share of profits under s.42(1), it is unnecessary to carry out any valuation exercise in relation to his share of the partnership assets, unlike the position where he seeks the payment of interest. In so holding, he declined to follow contrary views expressed by H.H. Judge Behrens in *Taylor v. Grier (No.3)*, May 12, 2003 (Lawtel 20/5/2003). It had been contended that Mr. Sandhu's share would, if an account were taken, be nil, and that accordingly he could not maintain a claim for a share of profits under the subsection.

Problems associated with the option under section 42(1)

See also *Sandhu v. Gill, supra*.   **25–29**

Capital profits

In *Emerson v. Estate of Emerson* [2004] 1 B.C.L.C. 575, CA, it was held that   **25–30** compensation received for the slaughter of livestock following the outbreak of foot and mouth disease constituted capital profits, so that s.42 had no application. See also *Gill v. Sandhu, supra*, at [7].

Remuneration for services

See also *Sandhu v. Gill, supra*, at [10]. Note that, whilst in *Emerson v. Estate of*   **25–31** *Emerson, supra*, an allowance was made in the amount of the loss borne by the surviving partner in carrying on the business, this was *not* a case falling with s.42.

4. DISTRIBUTION OF ASSETS AND ADJUSTMENT OF ACCOUNTS

Importance of agreement

NOTE 40. A note of the appeal in *Swift v. Dairywise Farms Ltd* now appears at   **25–42** [2003] 1 W.L.R. 1606.

CHAPTER 27

INSOLVENCY

1. INTRODUCTION

The statutory approach to insolvent partners and partnerships

27–06 It should be noted that in *Lancefield v. Lancefield* [2002] B.P.I.R. 1108, Neuberger J. ordered the winding up of an insolvent partnership on the application of a partner *without* the prior service of a petition. The circumstances were exceptional, *i.e.* following a dissolution it was clear that the business was not only insolvent but also unsaleable, so much so that a court appointed receiver had been discharged. A winding up order was perceived to be necessary to protect the position of third parties and, most significantly, there was no opposition to such an order. The decision, whilst attractive from a practical point of view, is difficult to reconcile with the provisions of the Insolvent Partnerships Order 1994.

NOTE 15. The Insolvent Partnerships Order 1994, art.4(1), Sch.1 have respectively been substituted by the Insolvent Partnerships (Amendment) (No.2) Order 2002 (SI 2002/2708), arts 5, 6.

NOTE 16. The Insolvent Partnerships Order 1994, art.6, Sch.2 have respectively been substituted by the Insolvent Partnerships (Amendment) Order 2005 (SI 2005/1516), arts 3, 7.

2. INSOLVENCY INVOLVING THE WINDING UP OF THE FIRM AS AN UNREGISTERED COMPANY

Winding up as an unregistered company under specific statutory jurisdiction

NOTE 27. The Insolvent Partnerships Order 1994, art.19(4) has been further amended by the Insolvent Partnerships (Amendment) (No.2) Order 2002, art.5. **27–07**

A. WINDING UP ORDER AGAINST FIRM WITHOUT CONCURRENT PETITIONS

See also the exceptional decision in *Lancefield v. Lancefield* [2002] B.P.I.R. 1108, noticed *supra*, para.27–06. *Quaere*, if a petition is presented against the firm and, only subsequently, petitions are presented against the partners, does this take the case out of this class. The point was raised but not, ultimately, answered in *HM Customs & Excise v. Jack Baars Wholesale* [2004] EWHC 18 (Ch) (Lawtel 16/1/04). **27–10**

Jurisdiction

See *Lancefield v. Lancefield, supra.* **27–11**

Grounds for petition

To this list must now be added the situation where, on the coming to an end of a moratorium under s.1A of the Insolvency Act 1986, no voluntary arrangement approved under *ibid.* Pt 1 is in effect: see *ibid.* 221(7)(d), as amended and applied by the Insolvent Partnerships Order 1994, art.7(1), (2), Sch.3, Pt 1, para.3 (as itself amended by the Insolvent Partnerships (Amendment) (No.2) Order 2002, art.8). **27–12**

Firm's inability to pay its debts **27–13**

NOTE 54. See also, as to going behind a judgment, *Re Thorogood (No.1)* [2003] B.P.I.R. 1468.

Who may present petition

To this list has now been added, in the case of creditor's, etc., petitions, a liquidator appointed in proceedings by virtue of Art.3(1) of Council Regulation (EC) No.1346/2000 of May 29, 2000 on insolvency proceedings (styled "the EC Regulation") and a temporary administrator within the meaning of Art.38 of that regulation: see the Insolvent Partnerships (Amendment) Order 2002 (SI 2002/1308), art.3, further amending the Insolvent Partnerships Order 1994, art.7(1). A petition on the ground referred to *supra*, para.27–12 may only be presented by one or more creditors: *ibid.* 221(7A), as amended and applied by the Insolvent Partnerships Order 1994, art.7(1), (2), Sch.3, Pt 1, para.3, as itself amended by the Insolvent Partnerships (Amendment) (No.2) Order 2002, art.8. **27–17**

NOTE 71. See *supra*, as to further amendments to art.7(1).

Consequences of presentation of petition

Avoidance of transactions

27–19   NOTE 88. See also, as to the width of the discretion under the Insolvency Act 1986, s.127, *Royal Bank of Scotland v. Bhardwaj* [2002] B.C.C. 57.

Appointment of provisional liquidator

27–21   NOTE 93. The Insolvency Rules 1986, r.4.25 has been amended by the Insolvency (Amendment) Rules 2002 (SI 2002/1307), r.6(5).

B. WINDING UP ORDER AGAINST FIRM WITH CONCURRENT PETITIONS AGAINST THE PARTNERS

27–27   Note the point raised, *supra*, para.27–10.

Grounds for petition against firm

27–29   An additional ground has now been added in the case of a creditor's petition, namely the situation where, on the coming to an end of a moratorium under s.1A of the Insolvency Act 1986, no voluntary arrangement approved under Pt 1 of the Act is in effect: see *ibid.* 221(8)(b), as amended and applied by the Insolvent Partnerships Order 1994, art.7(1), (2), Sch.4, Pt I, para.3, as itself amended by the Insolvent Partnerships (Amendment) (No.2) Order 2002, art.9(2).

Grounds for petition against corporate partner

27–30   A similar ground to that referred to *supra*, para.27–29 has been added in the case of creditors of the firm: see the Insolvency Act 1986 s.122(b), as amended and applied by the Insolvent Partnerships Order 1994, art.8(4), (5), (8), Sch.4, Pt II, para.6(a), as itself amended by the Insolvent Partnerships (Amendment) (No.2) Order 2002, art.9(3).

NOTE 33. Note that the Insolvent Partnerships Order 1994, art.10(6) has been substituted by the Insolvent Partnerships (Amendment) Order 2005, art.5(b).

Foreign corporate partner

27–31   NOTE 35. See *supra*, n.33.

Grounds for petition against individual partner

27–33   A similar ground to that referred to *supra*, para.27–29 has been added: see the Insolvency Act 1986 s.267(2), (2A), as amended and applied by the Insolvent Partnerships Order 1994, art.8(4), (5), (8), Sch.4, Pt II, para.6(a), as itself amended by the Insolvent Partnerships (Amendment) (No.2) Order 2002, art.9(4).

Minor or foreign partners

NOTE 46. See *supra*, n.33. **27–34**

Who may present petitions

Additional petitioners have been added to the Insolvent Partnerships Order 1994, **27–36** art.8(1) and to the Insolvency Act 1986, s.124(2), as amended and applied, in the same terms as are described *supra*, para.27–17 and the heading to the former article has been amended accordingly: see the Insolvent Partnerships (Amendment) Order 2002, arts 4, 5(4). Petitions on the grounds outlined, *supra*, paras 27–29, 27–30 and 27–33 may only be presented by a creditor of the firm.

Consequences of presentation of petitions

Consequences for the firm and any corporate partner

NOTE 65. Note that the Insolvent Partnerships Order 1994, art.10(6) has been **27–40** substituted by the Insolvent Partnerships (Amendment) Order 2005, art.5(b).

Consequences for an individual partner

NOTE 66. See *supra*, n.65. **27–41**

NOTE 68. The Insolvency Rules 1986, r.6.51 has been amended by the Insolvency (Amendment) Rules 2002 (SI 2002/1307), r.8(4).

The insolvency orders and their consequences

Order against the firm

NOTES 69, 70. See *supra*, n.65. **27–42**

Order against the corporate and individual partners

NOTE 74. See *supra*, n.65. **27–43**

3. INSOLVENCY NOT INVOLVING WINDING UP THE FIRM AS AN UNREGISTERED COMPANY

Consequences of presentation of joint petition

NOTE 6. The Insolvency Rules 1986, r.6.51 has been amended by the Insolvency **27–52** (Amendment) Rules 2002 (SI 2002/1307), r.8(4).

4. APPOINTMENT OF LIQUIDATORS AND TRUSTEES

Appointment of liquidator

Interim appointment

NOTE 25. Note that the Insolvent Partnerships Order 1994, art.10(6) has been **27–57** substituted by the Insolvent Partnerships (Amendment) Order 2005, art.5(b).

Appointment of trustee

27–60   NOTES 37, 40. See *supra*, n.25.

Subsequent order on concurrent petition

27–61   NOTES 41, 42. See *supra*, n.25.

Conflicts of interest

27–62   NOTE 43. See *supra*, n.25.

5. STATUS AND DUTIES OF THE PARTNERS IN THE WINDING UP OF A FIRM

Partners as officers

Disqualification orders

27–71   It should be noted that the same power is exercisable where a partnership enters administration: Company Directors Disqualification Act 1986, s.6(2)(a)(ii) as amended and applied by the Insolvent Partnerships Order 1994, art.16, Sch.8, as itself amended by the Insolvent Partnerships (Amendment) Order 2005, art.11(2)(a).

NOTE 79. The Company Directors' Disqualification Act 1986, Sch.1 has been further amended, in its application to partnerships, by the Insolvent Partnerships (Amendment) Order 2005, art.11(4).

6. SHARE OF AN INSOLVENT PARTNER WHEN FIRM NOT WOUND UP

Dissolution of firm and conduct of winding up

Dealings with partnership land

27–77   NOTE 10. Note also, in this context, *Barca v. Mears* [2005] B.P.I.R. 15.

Rights in relation to insolvent partner's share

27–78   NOTE 13. See also, as to the anti-deprivation principle, *Fraser v. Oystertec Plc* [2004] B.C.C. 233.

Expulsion prior to insolvency order

27–79   NOTE 18. The cross reference in this footnote should be to para.27–78, n.13.

7. SET-OFF AND MUTUAL CREDIT

NOTE 27. The Insolvency Rules 1986, r.4.90 has been substituted by the Insolvency (Amendment) Rules 2005 (SI 2005/527), r.23.   **27–81**

NOTE 31. See now the Insolvency Rules 1986, r.4.90(1), (8), as substituted by *ibid.*   **27–82**

NOTE 32. See also, as to what are mutual debts, *Secretary of State for Trade & Industry v. Frid* [2004] 2 A.C. 506, HL.

8. ADMINISTRATION OF THE ESTATES OF INSOLVENT FIRMS AND PARTNERS

Cases falling within the scope of the Insolvent Partnerships Order 1994

It should be noted that the Insolvency Act 1986, s.176A (as added by the Enterprise Act 2002, s.252), which seeks to secure a share of the assets for the unsecured creditors where property is subject to a floating charge, does not apply to the estate of an insolvent corporate partner wound up on a concurrent petition: see the Insolvent Partnerships Order 1994, art.8(5)(a), as amended by the Insolvent Partnerships Order 2005 (SI 2005/1516), art.4 (creditor's petition), and art.10(3)(a), as amended by *ibid.* art.5(a) (member's petition).   **27–91**

Priority of expenses

NOTE 55. Note that the Insolvent Partnerships Order 1994, art.10(6) has been substituted by the Insolvent Partnerships (Amendment) Order 2005, art.5(b).   **27–92**

Priority of debts in the joint and separate estates

NOTES 62, 67. See *supra*, n.55.   **27–93**

Joint and separate debts and estates

(b) Joint and separate estates

Agreements converting joint into separate estate and vice versa

NOTE 20. Note, as to the exercise of the discretion conferred by the Insolvency Act 1986, s.127, *Royal Bank of Scotland v. Bhardwaj* [2002] B.C.C. 57.   **27–112**

Exceptions to the general rule

NOTES 31, 32. See also *Doyle v. Saville* [2002] B.P.I.R. 947 (a decision under the Insolvency Act 1986, ss.339, 340).   **27–114**

NOTE 35. See also *IRC v. Hashmi* [2002] 2 B.C.L.C. 489, CA.

Priority and proof of debts

A. PROOF AGAINST THE JOINT ESTATE

(b) Rights of the partners

Where a partner may compete with his own creditors

(ii) *Distinct trades*

27–131 NOTE 9. Note that the Insolvent Partnerships Order 1994, art.10(6) has been substituted by the Insolvent Partnerships (Amendment) Order 2005, art.5(b).

9. VOLUNTARY ARRANGEMENTS WITH CREDITORS

Partnership voluntary arrangements

27–170 The provisions of the Insolvency Act 1986 as amended and applied to partnerships have been substantially amended by the Insolvent Partnerships (Amendment) (No.2) Order 2002 (SI 2002/2708), arts 4, 6 which substituted a new art.4(1) and Sch.1 in the Insolvent Partnerships Order 1994. All subsequent references (including those in the existing footnotes) to the latter Schedule are as so amended.

For the purposes of the amended provisions, an insolvent partnership will include such a partnership in relation to which a proposal for a voluntary arrangement may be made under Art.3 of Council Regulation (EC) No.1346/2000 of May 29, 2000 on insolvency proceedings: Insolvency Act 1986, s.1(4), as substituted and applied by the Insolvent Partnerships Order 1994, art.4(1), Sch.1, Pt I.

NOTES 18, 19, 23. The references to the Insolvent Partnerships Order 1994, Sch.1 should now be to *ibid.* Sch.1, Pt I.

Moratorium

27–171A An insolvent partnership which satisfies two or more of the qualifying conditions during the year ending with the date on which the application documents are filed or in the tax year ended next before that date may apply for a moratorium with a view to putting a voluntary arrangement in place: Insolvency Act 1986, Sch.A1, para.3(1), (2), as substituted and applied by the Insolvent Partnerships Order 1994, art.4(1), Sch.1, Pt II. Those qualifying conditions are that the firm's turnover must not be more than £2.8 million, its assets must not be more than £1.4 million and it must have not more than 50 employees on average during the relevant period: *ibid.* Sch.A1, para.3(3)–(7), as substituted and applied by *ibid.* However, a partnership will not be eligible for a moratorium if, predictably, it is not in a position to propose a PVA in the first place (as to which see para.27–171) or if an agricultural receiver has been appointed, a voluntary arrangement is already in effect, a provisional liquidator has been appointed or a moratorium has already been in force during the preceding 12 months and either no PVA had effect when it came to an end or any PVA has come to an end prematurely: *ibid.* Sch.A1, para.4(1), as substituted and applied by *ibid.*

A moratorium will protect the firm, *inter alia*, against the presentation of a winding up or joint bankruptcy petition, the making of a winding up or administration order, enforcement of any security over the partnership property, the commencement or continuation of proceedings (save with the leave of the court) or, more significantly, an application or order for a dissolution under s.35 of the Partnership Act 1890: *ibid.* Sch.A1, para.12(1), as substituted and applied by *ibid.*

The procedure for obtaining a moratorium is set out in *ibid.* Sch.A1, Pt II as applied by *ibid.* art.4(1) and read subject to *ibid.* s.1A(2)(b), (7), as substituted and applied by *ibid.*, art.4(1), Sch.1, Pt I.

Nominee's report

This requirement now only applies where the partners are *not* proposing to apply **27–172** for a moratorium under the Insolvency Act 1986, s.1A: see *ibid.* s.2(1), as substituted and applied by the Insolvent Partnerships Order 1994, art.4(1), Sch.1, Pt I. See, as to such applications, *supra*, para.17–171A. In his report the nominee must now state whether in his opinion the proposed PVA has a "reasonable prospect" of being approved and implemented: *ibid.* s.2(2)(a), as substituted and applied by *ibid.* A nominee may also be replaced where it is either impracticable or inappropriate for him to continue to act as such: *ibid.* s.2(5), as substituted and applied by *ibid.*

NOTES 29–32. The references to the Insolvent Partnerships Order 1994, Sch.1 should now be to *ibid.* Sch.1, Pt I.

Approval of the PVA

Where a creditor's debt is unliquidated or unascertained, it will, for voting **27–173** purposes, now be valued at £1, unless the chairman of the meeting agrees to put some higher value on it: Insolvency Rules 1986, r.1.17(3), as substituted by the Insolvency (Amendment) (No.2) Rules 2002 (SI 2002/2712), Sch., Pt I, para.8. And see also, as to the procedure at the meeting, *ibid.* r.1.17A, as substituted by *ibid.* It should also be noted that a person held out as a partner will no longer have a vote, with the revocation of *ibid.* rr.1.18(2) and 1.20(2) by *ibid.* Sch., Pt I, para.10.

If decisions to approve the PVA are taken at both the partners' and creditors' meetings in the same terms, the approval will naturally have effect: Insolvency Act 1986, s.4A(2), as substituted and applied by the Insolvent Partnerships Order 1994, Sch.1, Pt I. If decisions are taken in *different* terms, then a partner may apply to the court within 28 days and the court may thereupon order that the decision at the partners' meeting will have effect or make such other order as it sees fit: *ibid.* s.4A(3), (4), (6) as substituted and applied by *ibid.* If the firm is authorised under the Financial Services and Markets Act 2000, is an appointed representative thereunder or is carrying on a regulated business in breach of that Act, the Financial Services Authority is entitled to be heard on such an application: *ibid.* s.4A(5), (7), as substituted and applied by *ibid.* It is an offence to make false representations with a view to obtaining approval to a PVA: *ibid.* s.6A, as substituted and applied by *ibid.*

NOTES 33 to 36. The references to the Insolvent Partnerships Order 1994, Sch.1 should now be to *ibid.* Sch.1, Pt I.

NOTE 37. *Ibid.* r.1.17 has been substituted by *ibid.* and amended by the Insolvency (Amendment) Rules 2003 (SI 2003/1730), Sch.1, Pt I, para.5. *Ibid.* r.1.19 has been amended by the Insolvency (Amendment) (No.2) Rules 2002, Sch., Pt I, para.10.

Effect of approval

27–174 Approval of a PVA now also binds a person who would have been entitled to vote at the relevant meeting if he had had notice of it: Insolvency Act 1986, s.5(2)(b), as substituted and applied by the Insolvent Partnerships Order 1994, Sch.1, Pt I. However, such a person will still be entitled to any sum due to him when the PVA ceases to have effect provided that it did not come to an end prematurely: *ibid.* s.5(2A), as substituted and applied by *ibid.* He may also apply to the court on the same basis as is set out in n.45: *ibid.* s.6(2)(b), as substituted and applied by *ibid.*

NOTES 43 to 47. The references to the Insolvent Partnerships Order 1994, Sch.1 should now be to *ibid.* Sch.1, Pt I.

Company and individual voluntary arrangements

27–175 NOTE 49. The amendments referred to are now in force.

NOTE 55. See also *Re Goldspan Ltd* [2003] B.P.I.R. 93.

10. PARTNERSHIP ADMINISTRATORS AND ADMINISTRATION ORDERS

27–177 The company administration procedure was substantially reformed by the Enterprise Act 2002, s.248, Sch.16 and the revised procedure (as set out in the Insolvency Act 1986, Pt II, Sch.B1) is now applied to partnerships with appropriate modifications by the Insolvent Partnerships Order 1994, Pt III, art.6, Sch.2, as respectively substituted by the Insolvent Partnerships (Amendment) Order 2005 (SI 2005/1516), arts 3, 7, Sch.1. All subsequent references (including those in the existing footnotes) to art.6 of or Sch.2 to the 1994 Order are to that article or Schedule as so substituted.

Jurisdiction and power to appoint administrator

27–178 Under the new procedure, an administration order can only be made in relation to a partnership if the court is satisfied that the partnership is unable to pay its debts (see n.57 and the Insolvency Act 1986, Sch.B1, para.111(1), as substituted and applied by the Insolvent Partnerships Order 1994, art.6(1), Sch.2, para.41) and that the order is "reasonably likely to achieve the purpose of administration": Insolvency Act 1986, Sch.B1, para.11, as substituted and applied by *ibid.* art.6(1), Sch.2, para.5. The purpose of administration is set out in *ibid.* Sch.B1, para.3 (as applied by *ibid.* art.6(1)) and is, in essence, to rescue the partnership, to achieve a better result for its creditors than a winding up or to realise property with a view to making a distribution to one or more secured or preferential creditors.

It should be noted that an administrator of a partnership may also be appointed outside court by the holder of an agricultural floating charge or by the partners: *ibid.* Sch.B1, paras 2, 22, as substituted and applied by *ibid.* art.6(1), Sch.2, paras 2, 9. In the latter case, the appointment cannot be made within 12 months of a previous appointment: *ibid.* Sch.B1, para.23(2), as substituted and applied by *ibid.* art.6(1), Sch.2, para.23(2).

Moreover, no administrator can in general be appointed, by the court or otherwise, where the partnership is already in administration (*ibid.* Sch.B1, para.7, as substituted and applied by *ibid.* art.6(1), Sch.2, para.3) nor after an order has been made on a joint bankruptcy petition or for the winding up of the partnership as an unregistered company (*ibid.* Sch.B1, para.8, as substituted and applied by *ibid.* art.6(1), Sch.2, para.4).

Application for administration order or appointment of administrator

The application may now be made by partners, creditors or any combination of **27–179** them (see *ibid.* Sch.B1, para.12(1), as substituted and applied by *ibid.* art.6(1), Sch.2, para.6) and notice must, in addition to the persons listed in the text, also be given to anyone else who is entitled to appoint an administrator as the holder of an qualifying agricultural floating charge: see *ibid.* Sch.B1, paras 12(2), 14, as substituted and applied by *ibid.* art.6(1), Sch.2, paras 6, 7. As previously, where an agricultural receiver is already in place, the petition is likely to be dismissed unless his appointor consents: *ibid.* Sch.B1, para.39(1), as substituted and applied by *ibid.* art.6(1), Sch.2, para.15.

Where a person is entitled to appoint an administrator without a court order, he can only exercise that power after giving notice to the holder of any prior agricultural floating charge: *ibid.* Sch.B1, paras 15(1) (appointment by holder of agricultural charge), 26(1) (appointment by partners), as respectively substituted and applied by *ibid.* art.6(1), Sch.2, paras 8, 11. Notice can be dispensed with in the former case if the holder of the prior charge consents: *ibid.* Sch.B1, para.15(1)(b). Partners seeking to make an appointment must also file a copy of the notice with the court, accompanied by a statutory declaration containing the required information: *ibid.* Sch.B1, para.27, as substituted and applied by *ibid.* art.6(1), Sch.2, para.12. On making the appointment, partners must also file notice thereof together with a further statutory declaration and a statement by the administrator: *ibid.* Sch.B1, para.29, as substituted and applied by *ibid.* art.6(1), Sch.2, para.13.

Effect of actual or prospective administration

There is now a moratorium on most forms of insolvency proceedings and other **27–180,** legal process both when a partnership is actually in administration and when the **27–181** above procedures have been initiated in order to place a partnership into administration: see the Insolvency Act 1986, Sch.B1, paras 42–44, as applied and (where relevant) substituted by the Insolvent Partnerships Order 1994, art.6(1), Sch.2, paras 17, 18. Thus the position will in essence remain as set out in the text of paras 27–180, 27–181, save that a winding up order may still be made on public interest grounds or on a petition presented by the Financial Services Authority: *ibid.* Sch.B1, para.42(5). Any agricultural receiver previously appointed must vacate office once the partnership is in administration, and any receiver of part of the partnership property may be required by the administrator to vacate office: *ibid.* Sch.B1, para.41, as substituted and applied by *ibid.* art.6(1), Sch.2, para.16.

Powers and status of the administrator

27–182   The administrator continues to have wide powers to do anything "necessary or expedient for the management of the affairs, business and property of the [partnership]": *ibid.* Sch.B1, paras 59(1), 60, Sch.1, as applied by *ibid.* art.6(1) and, in the case of Sch.1, as substituted by *ibid.* Sch.2, para.43. As to calling meetings of the partners or creditors and seeking directions from the court, see *ibid.* Sch.B1, paras 62, 63, as applied by *ibid.*, and as to interference by the partners with the administrator's powers see *ibid.* paras 61, 64, as applied by *ibid.* and in the case of para.61, as substituted by *ibid.* Sch.2, para.22.

The status of the administrator as agent of the partnership is unchanged (*ibid.* Sch.B1, para.69(1), as substituted and applied by *ibid.* art.6(1), Sch.2, para.24), as is the partners' apparent absence of liability for the partnership debts and obligations incurred during the administration: see *ibid.* Sch.B1, para.69(2) as substituted and applied by *ibid.* (but note the distinction between the use of "members of the partnership" in para.69(1) and "officer of the partnership" in para.69(2)). As to the absence of any duty of care owed by the administrator to the unsecured creditors of a partnership, see *Oldham v. Kyrris* [2004] 1 B.C.L.C. 305, CA.

If the administrator believes that the partnership has no assets he must file a notice to that effect and this will bring his appointment to an end and, three months later, the partnership will be deemed to be dissolved, unless the court otherwise orders: *ibid.* para.84, as substituted and applied by *ibid.* art.6(1), Sch.2, para.28. As to the operation of this provision, see *Re Ballast Plc* [2005] 1 W.L.R. 1928 (a decision in relation to *ibid.* para.84 as applied to companies). Whether in adapting that provision the distinction between dissolution of a company and dissolution of a partnership was fully appreciated is open to doubt.

Part Six

LIMITED PARTNERSHIPS

CHAPTER 28

INTRODUCTION

Popularity of limited partnership

NOTE 30. See also *infra*, para.31–25.   **28–10**

Overseas limited partnerships

As to the agency based analysis on p.846, it may be that an analogy can be drawn **28–13**
with the decision in *Base Metal Trading Ltd v. Shamurin* [2005] 1 W.L.R. 1157,
CA, which concerned the proper law governing the equitable duty owed by a
director to his company. *Sed quaere.*

NOTE 48. The view set out in the text appears to be supported by John McDonnell
Q.C. in an article entitled "Know your Limit" in The Lawyer, June 27, 2005,
p.36. He refers to an example involving a Delaware limited partnership of which
Ivan Boesky was the general partner, although there seems to have been no
formal judicial decision on the liability issue.

CHAPTER 29

NATURE, FORMATION, DURATION AND REGISTRATION OF LIMITED PARTNERSHIPS

1. NATURE, FORMATION AND DURATION

Number of partners

29–02　All statutory restrictions on the size of limited partnerships were, with effect from December 21, 2002, removed by the Regulatory Reform (Reform of 20 Member Limit in Partnerships etc.) Order 2002 (SI 2002/3203), regs 2, 3.

2. REGISTRATION

Manner and place of registration

29–20　NOTE 70. See also *The Rewia* [1991] 2 Lloyd's Rep. 325; *King v. Crown Energy Trading AG*, *The Times*, March 14, 2003 (both decisions relating to the principal place of business of a company).

Effect of non-registration

29–25　A graphic example of such a case is to be found in *MacCarthaigh v. D* [1985] I.R. 73, where the limited partners had not made their capital contributions until some time *after* the firm had been registered.

3. LIMITED PARTNERSHIPS AND THE FINANCIAL SERVICES AND MARKETS ACT 2000

Limited partnership as a collective investment scheme

29–34　The status of a limited partnership as a collective investment scheme was expressly recognised by John Powell Q.C. (sitting as a deputy judge of the Chancery Division) in *Rose v. Lynx Express Ltd* [2004] 1 B.C.L.C. 397, at [5]. The point was not mentioned on appeal at [2004] 1 B.C.L.C. 455.

NOTE 9. The Financial Services and Markets Act 2000 (Collective Investment Schemes) Order 2001, Sch., para.9(1)(a) was substituted by the Financial Services and Markets Act 2000 (Miscellaneous Provisions) Order 2001 (SI 2001/3650), art.2(2).

NOTE 12. The Financial Services and Markets Act 2000 (Collective Investment Schemes) Order 2001 has been amended by the Financial Services and Markets Act 2000 (Miscellaneous Provisions) Order 2001 and the Financial Services and Markets Act 2000 (Collective Investment Schemes) (Amendment) Order 2005 (SI 2005/57).

NOTE 16. *Russell-Cooke Trust Co v. Elliott* is now reported at [2001] 1 All E.R. (D) 197; note also *Russell-Cooke Trust Co v. Prentis* [2003] 2 All E.R. 478, which was a similar case.

CHAPTER 30

THE RIGHTS AND OBLIGATIONS OF THE PARTNERS AS REGARDS THIRD PARTIES

2. THE LIABILITY OF PARTNERS FOR THE DEBTS AND OBLIGATIONS OF THE FIRM

B. LIMITED PARTNERS

(a) Extent and Duration of Liability

Extent of liability

30–09 NOTE 31. See also the Income and Corporation Taxes Act 1988, ss.118ZN, 118ZO (as added by the Finance Act 2005, s.73) and the Partnerships (Restrictions on Contributions to a Trade) Regulations 2005 (SI 2005/2017). Non-active *general* partners are now also subject to a similar regime: Income and Corporation Taxes Act 1988, ss.118ZE *et seq.* (as added by the Finance Act 2004, s.124(1) and amended by the Finance Act 2005, s.72(3)). Specific provisions govern the use of film-related losses: see *infra*, para.34–55B.

CHAPTER 31

THE RIGHTS AND OBLIGATIONS OF THE PARTNERS BETWEEN THEMSELVES

2. CAPITAL OF LIMITED PARTNERSHIPS

Initial capital and change of liability

The requirement that capital be contributed on entry is an inflexible one. In **31–05** *MacCarthaigh v. D* [1985] I.R. 73, the limited partners did not contribute their capital until some time *after* their date of entry. This meant that the firm's registration was defective and they accordingly forfeited their limited liability until such time as the contributions had been made: Limited Partnerships Act 1907, s.5. Of course, it would not be possible validly to register a limited partnership in which the limited partners have not contributed any capital at all.

3. SHARES IN LIMITED PARTNERSHIPS

Quantum: profits and losses

It is common to find that one or more partners benefit from a so-called "carried **31–13** interest", *i.e.* a share of profits which is dependent on a specified threshold of profitability having been achieved or rate of return received by other partners. Examples of typical structures are set out in the Memorandum of Understanding between the BVCA and the Inland Revenue on the income tax treatment of Venture Capital and Private Equity Limited Partnerships and Carried Interest dated July 22, 2003, section 7, reproduced at [2003] S.T.I. 1371, 1373 *et seq.*

5. PARTNERSHIP ACCOUNTS

Partnerships and Unlimited Companies (Accounts) Regulations 1993

It should be noted that where, as is often the case, all the partners are companies, **31–25** the accounts of the partnership will have to be drawn up in compliance with the

Partnerships and Unlimited Companies (Accounts) Regulations 1993 (SI 1993/1820): see further para.22–08. It is, however, provided by *ibid.* reg.2(2) that

"Any reference in these Regulations to the members of a qualifying partnership shall be construed, in relation to a limited partnership, as a reference to its general partner or partners."

In consequence, there has been speculation that a limited partnership comprising a corporate general partner and *individual* limited partners may be affected by the Regulations. In the current editor's view, this is to misread the above regulation which does not purport to amend the definition of "qualifying partnership" in *ibid.* regs 2(1), 3(1) but merely the subsequent references to its members in, *e.g.* *ibid.* regs 4(a), 5(1) (preparation and delivery of accounts). Had such an amendment not been made, the limited partners might have been obliged to undertake functions which would place them in breach of prohibition on participation in management contained in the Limited Partnerships Act 1907, s.6(1) and, thus, led to forfeiture of their limited liability.

Note that these Regulations are prospectively amended in minor respects by the Partnerships and Unlimited Companies (Accounts) (Amendment) Regulations 2005 (SI 2005/1987).

DISSOLUTION AND WINDING UP

2. DISSOLUTION BY THE COURT

A. JURISDICTION TO DISSOLVE A LIMITED PARTNERSHIP

Winding up as an unregistered company

NOTE 20. The Insolvent Partnerships Order 1994, arts 7(1), 8(1) have respec- **32–08**
tively been amended by the Insolvent Partnerships (Amendment) Order 2002 (SI
2002/1308), arts 3, 4.

Firms providing financial services

NOTE 28. The Insolvent Partnerships Order 1994, art.19(4) has been further **32–09**
amended by the Insolvent Partnerships (Amendment) (No.2) Order 2002 (SI
2002/2708), art.5.

B. GROUNDS FOR DISSOLUTION BY THE COURT

Mental disorder of a general or limited partner

Once the Mental Health Act 1983, s.96 has been repealed by the Mental Capacity **32–10**
Act 2005, Sch.7, there will be no special power to order a dissolution otherwise
than pursuant to the Partnership Act 1890: see *supra*, para.24–47.

Part Seven

TAXATION

CHAPTER 34

INCOME TAX

1. INTRODUCTION

The development of partnership taxation

The schedule based approach to the taxation of income has been reformulated and is now set out, *inter alia*, in the Income Tax (Trading and Other Income) Act 2005, which came into force on April 6, 2005 and has effect for income tax purposes for the tax year 2005/2006 and subsequent years: *ibid.* s.883(1). The new provisions in large measure replace the provisions of the Income and Corporation Taxes Act 1988 and the Finance Act 1998 relating to the taxation of trading income (formerly Schedule D), albeit that certain of the provisions remain in place in an amended form for the purposes of corporation tax. Thus, the formerly key provisions contained in the Income and Corporation Taxes Act 1988, s.111 now apply for such purposes in a substantially truncated form: see the amendments effected by the Income Tax (Trading and Other Income) Act 2005, Sch.1, para.92, Sch.3. **34–01, 34–03**

The application of the Taxes Management Act 1970 and the Capital Allowances Act 2001 is, however, unaffected, whilst the charge to tax on employees (formerly Schedule E) is now contained in the Income Tax (Earnings and Pensions) Act 2003.

All references to the Revenue should now be read as references to the newly constituted HM Revenue & Customs: see the Commissioners for Revenue and Customs Act 2005, s.4.

2. TAX TREATMENT OF PARTNERSHIPS

Partnerships and the Income Tax (Trading and Other Income) Act 2005

The main statutory provisions, which in large measure replicate the provisions formerly contained in the Income and Corporation Taxes Act 1988, s.111, are **34–04** now to be found in the Income Tax (Trading and Other Income) Act 2005, Pt 9. The following table of equivalence in relation to the provisions quoted in this paragraph may assist:

ICTA 1988	IT(TOI)A 2005
s.111(1)	ss.847, 848
s.111(2)	s.849
s.111(3)	s.850
s.111(4)	ss.852, 853
s.111(7)	s.851
s.111(8)	ss.854, 855
s.111(10)	s.847(2)(b)
s.111(11)	s.847(3)(b)
s.111(12)	s.854(6).

34–05, 34–06 The summary in these paragraphs still, in essence, holds good under the new provisions, although they do not apply as regards the charge to corporation tax on corporate partners. The Income and Corporation Taxes Act 1988, s.111(1) still applies for such purposes: see *supra*, paras 34–01, 34–03. It should, however, be noted that the legislation now refers to a partner's "notional trade" and "notional business" in place of the two former "deemed" trades.

NOTE 12. See the Income Tax (Trading and Other Income) Act 2005, s.849(1), (2).

NOTE 13. *ibid.* s.850.

NOTES 14, 15. *ibid.* s.852. This is described as the partner's "notional trade".

NOTE 16. As defined in *ibid.* s.854(6).

NOTE 17. *ibid.* s.854. This is described as the partner's "notional business".

NOTE 18. *ibid.* ss.852(2)–(5), 854(2), (4).

Partnership agreements and the Revenue

(a) *Existence of partnership*

34–08 See the decision of the Supreme Court of Canada in *Backman v. R*, 3 I.T.L. Rep. 647, regarding the requirements for the existence of a partnership for tax purposes. And note also *Kings v. King* [2004] S.T.C. (SCD) 186.

34–10 NOTE 32. This section (as amended) still applies. See also *ibid.* s.118ZE, as added by the Finance Act 2004, s.124(1).

34–11 NOTE 33. See also *Barclays Mercantile Business Finance Ltd v. Mawson* [2005] 1 A.C. 684, HL; *I.R.C. v. Scottish Provident Institution* [2004] 1 W.L.R. 3172, HL.

Note 34. See also *New Angel Court Ltd v. Adam* [2004] 1 W.L.R. 1988, CA.

Note 36. See now the Income Tax (Earnings and Pensions) Act 2003, s.49(1)(c).　**34–12**
And see *Usetech Ltd v. Young* [2004] S.T.C. 1671. Note also the Social Security
Contributions (Intermediaries) Regulations 2000 (SI 2000/727), as amended, and
Synaptek Ltd v. Young [2003] S.T.C. 543; *Future Online Ltd v. Foulds* [2005]
S.T.C. 198; also *Tilbury Consulting Ltd v. Gittins (No.2)* [2004] S.T.C. (SCD) 72;
Netherlane Ltd v. York [2005] S.T.C. (SCD) 305.

Note 37. See now the Income Tax (Earnings and Pensions) Act 2003, s.52(2).

Note 38. See now *ibid.* s.50(1). Revised guidance on IR 35 was issued by HM
Revenue & Customs on June 8, 2005: see [2005] S.T.I. 1048.

Partnerships as settlements

It is now clear that, in the case of husband and wife partnerships (and other　**34–12A**
analogous situations), HM Revenue & Customs are likely to seek to apply the
settlement legislation (see the Income Tax (Trading and Other Income) Act 2005,
ss.620, 624, 625) for income tax purposes, unless both spouses are active
participants in the business: see I.R. Tax Bulletins 64 (April 2003) and 69
(February 2004, reproduced at [2004] S.T.I. 460) and the Guidance at [2004]
S.T.I. 2369; and see also [2003] S.T.I. 1921, 2246; [2004] S.T.I. 2446. Such an
argument succeeded in the case of a corporate structure in *Jones v. Garnett*, *The
Times*, May 17, 2005. As in the case of IR 35 (see para.34–12), this does not
mean that the partnership does not exist, but may result in the whole of the
partnership profits being taxed in the hands of only one spouse *qua* settlor.

(b) *Date of commencement or dissolution of the partnership*

Note 46. The section will be repealed as from April 6, 2006: Finance Act 2004,　**34–17**
Sch.42, Pt 3.

3. Method of Assessment

Partnership returns, etc.

Note 47. Now HM Revenue & Customs: see the Commissioners for Revenue　**34–18**
and Customs Act 2005, s.4.

Note 49. The reference in the last line should be to s.12AA(11)(b).

Note 52. The reference in the last line should be to Ray, *Partnership Taxation*,
para.11.4.

Tax no longer a joint debt

Note 57. See now the Income Tax (Trading and Other Income) Act 2005,　**34–19**
s.852(1). As to the notional business treated as carried on in relation to other
untaxed income, see *ibid.* s.854.

Ascertainment and apportionment of profits

The current year basis

34–20 NOTE 62. See now the Income Tax (Trading and Other Income) Act 2005, s.853(1), applying *ibid.* s.198(1). As to the position in the first and second tax years, see *ibid.* ss.199, 200.

NOTE 63. See *ibid.* ss.200(4), 201.

NOTE 64. Note also *Small v. Mars (UK) Ltd* [2005] S.T.C. 958.

NOTE 65. This is now, in any event, required under *ibid.* s.25(1). The "true and fair" approach has been abandoned in favour of "generally accepted accounting practice".

Ascertainment of partners' profit shares

34–21 The Income Tax (Trading and Other Income) Act 2005, s.850(1) specifically states that a partner's share of any profit or loss will be determined in accordance with the firm's "profit-sharing arrangements" during the relevant accounting period. This expression includes both profit sharing and loss sharing ratios, where they differ: *ibid.* s.850(6). However, there is now provision to avoid the creation of a notional loss for one or more partners during a period when the partnership as a whole makes a profit. In such a case, the loss-making partners' shares are deemed to be nil and the remaining partners' profit shares are adjusted accordingly: *ibid.* s.850(2), (3). Similarly, where a notional profit is shared by one or more partners during a period when the partnership has made an overall loss: *ibid.* s.850(4), (5). In applying this rule, account can be taken of any partner even if he or it is not subject to income tax: see the definition of "partner" in *ibid.* s.850(6).

Note the exceptional decision in *Chartered Accountants' Firm v. Braisby* [2005] S.T.C. (SCD) 389, where application of an agreed profit sharing adjustment resulted in the "payment" of negative salaries to some of the partners, as part of the overall profit allocation.

Accounting basis: "generally accepted accounting practice"

34–22 As will be apparent from the heading, the "true and fair" approach adopted by the Finance Act 1998, s.42 was abandoned in favour of generally accepted accounting practice with effect from July 24, 2002 (see the Finance Act 2002, s.103(5)) and the same approach is now adopted in the Income Tax (Trading and Other Income) Act 2005, s.25(1). As a result, it is now, *inter alia*, necessary to reflect the approach advocated in Application Note G (entitled "Revenue Recognition") to Financial Reporting Standard 5 ("Reporting the Substance of Transactions"), which was issued by the Accounting Standards Board in November 2003, and the subsequent advice issued by the Urgent Issues Taskforce on March 10, 2005 (see Abstract 40, "Revenue recognition and service contracts"), in terms of the recognition of income. See further *supra*, paras 21–04, 22–07. To this extent, in accounts for a period ending on or after June 22, 2005, firms may have to recognise income attributable to partners' work in progress before it is actually billed, unlike the former position described in this paragraph. This will inevitably lead to an adjustment charge under *ibid.* ss.226 *et seq.*

Given the terms of Application Note G, it is in future likely to be difficult for a firm to justify preparing its accounts on some other basis, even if an adjustment is made for tax purposes. That is not to say that management and other internal accounts cannot be prepared on any basis the firm sees fit.

It is still clear that there is no audit requirement: Income Tax (Trading and Other Income) Act 2005, s.25(2)(b).

Work in progress spreading adjustment

The regime described in this paragraph is now largely historic, although many   **34–23** firms are still subject to the spreading adjustment charge during the balance of the 10-year period. No such adjustment is now permissible on a change of accounting basis under the Income Tax (Trading and Other Income) Act 2005, in respect of which a charge on the appropriate adjustment income will be made under *ibid.* ss.226 *et seq.*

Directors' fees

Schedule E no longer exists: see now the Income Tax (Earnings and Pensions)   **34–24** Act 2003.

NOTE 86. See now the Income Tax (Trading and Other Income) Act 2005, s.849.

NOTE 87. Extra-Statutory Concession A37 was revised in January 2004.

Other sources of income

The reference to the Taxes Act in the last line should be read as a reference to the   **34–25** Income Tax (Trading and Other Income) Act 2005.

NOTE 88. See now the Income Tax (Trading and Other Income) Act 2005, s.851.

NOTE 89. See now *ibid.* s.854(6).

NOTE 90. See now *ibid.* ss.854, 855. This is now described as the "notional business" as opposed to a second deemed trade: *ibid.* The former Sch.A charge is now imposed under *ibid.* ss.263 *et seq.* The Revenue Interpretation referred to is RI 137.

NOTE 91. The former Sch.F charge is now imposed under *ibid.* ss.328 *et seq.*

Treatment of payments to partners

In *Chartered Accountants' Firm v. Braisby* [2005] S.T.C. (SCD) 389 certain of   **34–26** the partners were even treated as receiving negative salaries, as a result of an agreed adjustment to one partner's profit share. In terms of the overall profit, this naturally made no difference.

Note 95. The former Schedule E charge is now imposed under the Income Tax (Earnings and Pensions) Act 2003. As to possibility (a), see now *ibid.* ss.48 *et seq.* and, as to possibility (b), see now *ibid.* ss.44 *et seq.*

Note 96. See now the Income Tax (Trading and Other Income) Act 2005, s.34(1)(a).

Earned income

34–27 Note 3. The Income and Corporation Taxes Act 1988, s.833(4)(c) has been amended by the Income Tax (Trading and Other Income) Act 2005, Sch.1, para.338(3)(b).

Note 5. See *supra*, n.3. The subsection now refers to Pt 2 of the 2005 Act, whereas dividends are chargeable under *ibid.* ss.328 *et seq.*

Deductibility of expenses incurred by individual partners

34–28 Note 6. See now the Income Tax (Trading and Other Income) Act 2005, s.34(1)(a).

Loans taken out by partners

34–29 Note 9. The Income and Corporation Taxes Act 1988, s.353(1) has been further amended by the Income Tax (Trading and Other Income) Act 2005, Sch.1, para.152. The reference to the Finance Act 1988 should now merely be to Sch.6, para.3.3(i), (4): Finance Act 2002, Sch.25, para.59, Sch.40, Pt 3(12).

Note 14. s.117(1), (2) has been further amended by the Finance Act 2005, ss.72(1), 78(1), Sch.11, Pt 2(4).

Pre-owned assets charge

34–30A This charge, which was introduced by s.84 of the Finance Act 2004 with effect from the 2005/06 year of assessment, will have no impact on the *partnership* profits, but should nevertheless be noted in the present context. Thus, where an individual partner disposes of land or a chattel (or an interest therein) but seeks to retain the occupation or use of that asset through his membership of the partnership, he may be subject to a charge to income tax by reference to the assessed rental value of the land or an assumed rate of interest on the value of the chattel, less any amounts which he is legally obliged to pay in respect of that occupation or use: Finance Act 2004, Sch.15, paras 3(1), (2)(a)(i), 4 (land) and 6(1), (2)(a)(i), 7 (chattels); also the Charge to Income Tax by Reference to Enjoyment of Property Previously Owned Regulations 2005 (SI 2005/724), reg.4. Similarly, where he directly or indirectly funds the acquisition of the relevant land or chattel: *ibid.* Sch.15, paras 3(2)(a)(ii), (3), 6(2)(a)(ii), (3).

However, the above regime will not apply where the original disposal was of the whole of a partner's interest in the relevant property (apart from any rights reserved) under an arm's length transaction or what would be such a transaction if he was not treated as connected with his co-partners (see *ibid.* Sch.15, para.10(1)(a)) or of part of his interest under such a transaction, provided that the consideration is not in the form of money or readily convertible assets: see *ibid.* Sch.15, para.14; the Charge to Income Tax by Reference to Enjoyment of Property Previously Owned Regulations 2005, reg.5. On the latter basis, HM Revenue & Customs accept that, where a partner receives full, albeit non-monetary, consideration for a disposal of a share in the partnership to an incoming partner (even if they are connected otherwise than as partners), the exclusion will apply: see the partnership example in the Inland Revenue Press Release "Pre-owned assets—technical guidance" dated March 17, 2005, Appendix 1 (reproduced at [2005] S.T.I. 630, 645). The regime will also not apply where the transaction involves or would, but for some available exemption, involve a gift with a reservation for inheritance tax purposes (*ibid.* Sch.15, para.11(5); and see *infra*, para.36–40 *et seq.*). It is also possible to avoid the charge by *voluntarily* electing to apply the gift with a reservation rules: *ibid.* Sch.15, para.21. The other exceptions and exemptions are unlikely to have a significant impact in the present context: see *ibid.* Sch.15, paras 10(1), (2), 13.

A similar regime applies in the case of intangible property comprised in a **34–30B** settlement where the settlor retains an interest: *ibid.* Sch.15, paras 8, 9. It has already been seen that, in some circumstances, a partnership may be regarded as a settlement: see *supra*, para.34–12A. HM Revenue & Customs have confirmed that the arrangement of mutual life insurance policies to fund the payment out of a deceased partner's share is excluded, provided that the partner is not a beneficiary of his own policy: see the Inland Revenue Press Release "Pre-owned assets guidance amended" dated April 1, 2005 (reproduced at [2005] S.T.I. 724).

4. COMMENCEMENT, CESSATION AND CONTINUANCE

Taxation of new partnership or incoming partner

This separate trade is, as previously noted, now styled the "notional trade". Note **34–33** that special rules may apply where the first (or later) accounting date chosen by the firm falls on March 31 or between April 1 and April 4 (see the Income Tax (Trading and Other Income) Act 2005, ss.208, 209) or where a variable accounting date is adopted (see *ibid.* ss.211–213).

NOTE 23. See now the Income Tax (Trading and Other Income) Act 2005, ss.199, 202(2), 852(2), (3).

NOTE 24. This expression is no longer adopted. In the heading to *ibid.* s.199 it is styled "first tax year".

NOTE 25. *ibid.* ss.199(1). Special rules apply where the notional trade is commenced before April 1 (*ibid.* s.210(2)) or after March 31 (*ibid.* s.210(4)).

NOTE 26. *ibid.* ss.198(1), 200(1), (3). As to the position where there is no accounting date during that year, see *ibid.* s.210(3).

NOTE 27. *ibid.* ss.200(1), (2).

NOTE 28. *ibid.* s.198(1).

NOTE 29. *ibid.* ss.214, 215. As to subsequent changes, see *ibid.* ss.216 *et seq.*

34–34 This right is now also extended to the intensive rearing of livestock or fish on a commercial basis for food production and to a trade the profits of which are derived from wholly or mainly from "creative works": Income Tax (Trading and Other Income) Act 2005, s.221(2)(b), (c), (3).

NOTE 30. See now the Income Tax (Trading and Other Income) Act 2005, s.221(1).

NOTE 31. *ibid.* ss.222–224. As to the timing of claims for relief, see *ibid.* ss.222(5), 225(4).

NOTE 32. See now *ibid.* s.852(4)–(6).

NOTE 33. *ibid.* s.222(4)(a). Similarly, in case of the "creative works" category, the years in which the trade first qualifies or ceases to be qualified are excluded: *ibid.* s.222(4)(b).

Overlap profits

34–35 Note that the exception mentioned in the text in the case of a basis period of more than 12 months' duration applies only following a change of accounting date: Income Tax (Trading and Other Income) Act 2005, s.220. In any other case, the period will be only 12 months: see *ibid.* ss.198(1), 200(3), 201(1).

As noted *supra*, paras 34–05, 34–06, the second deemed trade referred to is now styled the "notional business".

NOTE 34. See now the Income Tax (Trading and Other Income) Act 2005, s.200(2).

NOTE 35. See now *ibid.* s.204.

NOTE 36. *ibid.* s.205.

NOTES 37, 38. See *supra*.

NOTE 39. *ibid.* s.854.

NOTE 40. *ibid.* s.856(2), (3).

Taxation of discontinued partnership or outgoing partner

Outgoing partners

Special provision is no longer made as to the position of a partner who leaves the **34–36** firm in the year following that in which he joined. If he joins and leaves in the *same* tax year, the basis period will be the period whilst he remained a partner: Income Tax (Trading and Other Income) Act 2005, s.202(2).

Moreover, the 2005 Act no longer contains a specific provision regarding the assessment of tax where a partner has died.

NOTE 42. See now the Income Tax (Trading and Other Income) Act 2005, s.852(1). This is now styled the "notional trade": *ibid.*

NOTE 43. *ibid.* s.852(4)(a).

NOTE 44. There is, however, now no equivalent to the Income and Corporation Taxes Act 1988, s.113(1), (2) to point to in such a case. The circumstances supposed would not seem to fall within Income Tax (Trading and Other Income) Act 2005, s.852(5), which refers to the "actual trade", but the reasoning set out in the latter part of the footnote still holds good. Might the outgoing partners in such a case be regarded as the same "firm" as the partnership they have left? See further *infra*, para.34–37.

NOTE 47. *ibid.* s.202(1).

NOTE 48. *ibid.* s.202(2).

NOTE 49. This is no longer applicable: see *supra.*

NOTE 50. The Taxes Management Act 1970, s.40(1) still applies, but the Income and Corporation Taxes Act 1988, s.113(6) is not replicated in the 2005 Act.

Continuing partners

It should again be noted that a partner will now be treated as a carrying on a **34–37** "notional trade" and, if appropriate, a separate "notional business": see *supra*, paras 34–05, 34–06. Although the current editor believes that the position remains as set out in the text, there is now no specific provision equivalent to the Income and Corporation Taxes Act 1988, s.113(1) (as amended). The absence of any form of cessation would seem to follow from the Income Tax (Trading and Other Income) Act 2005, ss.852(1), (4)(a) (notional trade) and 854(1), (4)(a) (notional business), subject only to what meaning is ascribed to the expression "a firm" in *ibid.* ss.852(1), 854(1). Significantly, a firm is not regarded as an entity separate and distinct from the partners who for the time being make it up (*ibid.* s.848), but this would seem to let in the analysis set out at the beginning of the original text of this paragraph. The drafting of the new legislation is, in this respect, less than satisfactory.

The existence of the notional business is clearly not affected by changes in the source of its income or, indeed, by an absence of income from that source: *ibid.* s.854(3).

There will also be a permanent cessation and commencement of both a partner's notional trade and business if the firm's *actual* trade is carried on outside the UK and he becomes non-resident: *ibid.* ss.852(6), 854(5).

NOTE 53. This is no longer applicable: see *supra.*

Dissolution and cessation of trade

34–38   Again, there will be a cessation of both a partner's notional trade and business in such a case.

NOTE 57. See now the Income Tax (Trading and Other Income) Act 2005, ss.852(4)(b), 854(4)(b). And see *supra*, paras 34–36, n.44, 34–37.

Mergers

34–39   NOTE 59. Note, however, that SP9/86 has not been updated to reflect the demise of the Income and Corporation Taxes Act 1988, s.113. Nevertheless, the current editor has no reason to suppose that a change of practice is heralded in this area.

Hiving-off operations and demergers

34–40,   The concept of the deemed discontinuance has no place under the Income Tax
34–41   (Trading and Other Income) Act 2005.

As previously noted, each partner will now be treated as carrying on a notional trade (as opposed to a deemed trade) and, if appropriate, a notional business: see *supra*, paras 34–05, 34–06. The effect of a change in the scope of the latter has already been seen *supra*, para.34–37.

NOTE 64. See *supra*, para.34–39, n.59.

Overlap profits

34–42   NOTE 66. See now the Income Tax (Trading and Other Income) Act 2005, s.204.

NOTE 67. *ibid.* s.205.

Work in progress spreading adjustment

34–43   As noted *supra*, para.34–23, this is increasingly of only historic importance.

Post-cessation receipts

34–44   Each partner is now treated as carrying on a notional trade (see *supra*, paras 34–05, 34–06) and the charge to tax on post-cessation receipts is imposed under the Income Tax (Trading and Other Income) Act 2005, Pt 2, Chap.18. The concept of the deemed discontinuance has now completely gone, but the consequences of a transfer of the right to receive sums due from one firm to another is now governed by *ibid.* s.98. The specific provision regarding debts taken over has not been retained, save as regards companies (see the Income and Corporation Taxes Act 1988, s.89, as substituted by the Income Tax (Trading and Other Income) Act 2005, Sch.1, para.65), but see, generally, s.35(1) of the latter Act, as regards bad and doubtful debts.

NOTE 70. See now the Income Tax (Trading and Other Income) Tax Act 2005, ss.243–245.

NOTES 71–73. See the text *supra*.

Trading stock

In the case of a sale to a connected person where the open market value of the stock exceeds both the acquisition value (as defined) and, if greater, the actual purchase price, it is now possible for both parties to elect to use the greater of those amounts: see the Income Tax (Trading and Other Income) Act 2005, s.178.   **34–45**

NOTE 74. As previously noted, this is no longer a relevant concept. Note that, in this instance, the Income Tax (Trading and Other Income) Act 2005, s.173(3) provides specifically that no revaluation is required when there is a change in the persons carrying on the trade.

NOTE 75. *ibid.* s.174.

NOTE 76. *ibid.* ss.175(2), 176. As to the meaning of connected persons, see *ibid.* s.179, which, *inter alia*, applies the test set out in the Income and Corporation Taxes Act 1988, s.839 (as amended). A partner will clearly be connected with a firm of which he is a member, as will two firms with a common partner: see the Income Tax (Trading and Other Income) Act 2005, s.179(b), (d); also the Income and Corporation Taxes Act 1988, s.839(4).

NOTE 77. See the Income Tax (Trading and Other Income) Act 2005, s.177.

NOTE 78. *ibid.* ss.173(1), 175(4).

NOTE 79. The difference in wording between *ibid.* ss.175(4) and 177(2) has, in substance, been retained.

Work in progress

NOTE 80. See now the Income Tax (Trading and Other Income) Act 2005, s.183.   **34–46**

NOTE 81. As previously noted, this is no longer a relevant concept.

NOTE 82. *ibid.* s.184.

NOTE 83. *ibid.* s.185. Post-cessation receipts are now charged to tax under *ibid.* Pt 2, Chap.18. See further *ibid.* s.252.

Post-cessation expenditure

34–47 NOTE 84. The Income and Corporation Taxes Act 1988, s.109(4) has been further amended by the Income Tax (Trading and Other Income) Act 2005, Sch.1, para.89, Sch.3 and (for corporation tax purposes only) by the Finance Act 2005, Sch.4, para.6. The Income and Corporation Taxes Act 1988, s.89, as substituted by the Income Tax (Trading and Other Income) Act 2005, Sch.1, para.65, now applies only as regards companies.

NOTE 86. The Income and Corporation Taxes Act 1988, s.109A(3) has been repealed by the Income Tax (Trading and Other Income) Act 2005, Sch.1, para.89(1), Sch.3. See now *ibid.* s.250.

5. CAPITAL ALLOWANCES AND LOSSES

Capital allowances

34–48 In lieu of the former requirement that there should have been no deemed discontinuance is a requirement that the change in the firm does not involve all of the partners permanently ceasing to carry on the qualifying activity: Capital Allowances Act 2001, ss.263(1A)(a), 558(1A)(a), as added by the Income Tax (Trading and Other Income), Act 2005, Sch.1, paras 549(3), 571. Where the change does have that effect, there will be a deemed sale as described in the text: see the Capital Allowances Act 2001, ss.265(1A)(a), 559(1A)(a) as added by *ibid.* Sch.1, paras 550(3), 572(3).

NOTE 88. Now a "notional trade": see the Income Tax (Trading and Other Income) Act 2005, s.852(1).

NOTE 89. *ibid.* s.850. See further *supra*, para.34–21.

Changes in firm

34–49 NOTE 90. As noted *supra*, para.34–48, this is not longer a relevant concept.

NOTE 91. See the amendments referred to *supra*, para.34–48.

NOTE 92. See *ibid.* The dredging allowance exception has now gone: the Capital Allowances Act 2001, s.488(3)(a) has been amended by the Income Tax (Trading and Other Income) Act 2005, Sch.1, para.568.

NOTE 95. Capital Allowances Act 2001, s.570 has been amended by the Finance Act 2001, Sch.19, Pt II, para.6, the Finance Act 2005, Sch.6, para.8 and the Commissioners for Revenue and Customs Act 2005, Sch.4, para.83(1).

Machinery and plant

NOTE 1. Now a "notional trade": see the Income Tax (Trading and Other Income) **34–50**
Act 2005, s.852(1) and *supra*, paras 34–05, 34–06.

Losses

NOTE 5. The Income and Corporation Taxes Act 1988, s.382(3) has been **34–52**
amended by the Income Tax (Trading and Other Income) Act 2005, Sch.1,
para.158, Sch.3.

NOTE 7. See now the Income Tax (Trading and Other Income) Act 2005,
s.850(1), (6). Note, however, the adjustments made when one or more partners
suffer a loss in a year when the firm makes an overall profit and vice versa: *ibid.*
s.850(2)–(5). See also *supra*, para.34–21.

NOTE 9. This is now styled his "notional trade": *ibid.* s.852(1).

NOTE 10. This is now styled his "notional business": *ibid.* s.854(1).

NOTE 11. The Income and Corporation Taxes Act 1988, s.384A has been
amended by the Income Tax (Trading and Other Income) Act 2005, Sch.1,
para.160. There are now the following additional restrictions on the use of losses
(adopting sequential numbering): (5) Income and Corporation Taxes Act 1988,
s.118ZE (as added by the Finance Act 2004, s.124(1) and amended by the
Income Tax (Trading and Other Income) Act 2005, Sch.1, para.98 and the
Finance Act 2005, s.72(3), Sch.11, Pt 2(4)) (non-active general partners in a
limited partnership); and (6) *ibid.* s.118ZL (as added by the Finance Act 2004,
s.125 and amended by the Income Tax (Trading and Other Income) Act 2005,
Sch.1, para.101)) (exploitation of films). *Ibid.* s.392 has been substituted by the
Income Tax (Trading and Other Income) Act 2005, Sch.1, para.168. And see also
the additional charges noted *infra*, paras 34–55B, 34–55C.

NOTE 12. The Finance Act 1991, s.72 has been further amended by the Finance
Act 2002, s.48(1).

NOTE 13. The proposition in the latter part of this footnote would still appear to
hold good under the Income Tax (Trading and Other Income) Act 2005,
ss.852(1), 854(1), which apply only for the purposes of *ibid.* Pt 2, Chap.15 (basis
periods).

NOTE 14. Now styled the "notional trade" and the "notional business": see *ibid.* **34–53**
ss.852(2), 854(2).

NOTE 15. As to whether a trade is being carried on on a commercial basis, see
also *Walsh v. Taylor* [2004] S.T.C. (SCD) 48. See also the further restrictions on
this relief noted *supra*, para.34–52, n.11.

Pre-trading expenditure

34–54 NOTE 16. Now the "notional trade" and, where relevant, the "notional business": Income Tax (Trading and Other Income) Act 2005, ss.852(1), 854(1). See further, *supra*, paras 24–05, 34–06.

NOTE 17. See now *ibid.* s.57.

Limited and non-participating partners

34–55 It should be noted that, in computing a partner's capital contribution for this purpose, HM Revenue & Customs now have power, by regulation, to exclude specific items from qualifying as part of such a partner's contribution: see the Income and Corporation Taxes Act 1988, s.117(5) (as added by the Finance Act 2005, s.73(2)), applying the power under *ibid.* s.118ZN (as added by *ibid.* s.73(1)). That power has been exercised in the Partnerships (Restrictions on Contributions to a Trade) Regulations 2005 (SI 2005/2017) so as to exclude loans taken out in connection with the financing of the contribution provided that one of a number of conditions is satisfied: *ibid.* reg.4. Those conditions are, in essence, designed to catch any arrangement under which the loan is (or is likely to be) paid off, assumed or released by another person or where the loan is made otherwise than on arm's length terms viewed over a 5-year period. In such a case the financial costs of repaying the loan or the outstanding capital liability thereunder will be excluded from the contribution. A similar exclusion applies where the financial cost of making the contribution is to be (or is in fact) reimbursed by another person: *ibid.* reg.5. There are limited exceptions specified in *ibid.* reg.6, which would appear to include, *inter alia*, the situation where a loan is to be repaid out of the contributing partner's profit share: *ibid.* reg.6(c).

Where relief has been given to the extent of a partner's contribution and that contribution is subsequently reduced, the excess relief can now be recovered from him by a charge under the Finance Act 2005, s.74.

NOTE 21. Now the "notional trade" and, where relevant, the "notional business": Income Tax (Trading and Other Income) Act 2005, ss.852(1), 854(1). See further, *supra*, paras 24–05, 34–06. As to the proposition in the latter part of the footnote, see *supra*, para.34–52, n.13.

NOTE 22. See the text, *supra*.

Non-active general partners

34–55A Where a partner who is either a general partner within the meaning of the Limited Partnerships Act 1907, s.4(2) or a partner in a general partnership does not devote a significant amount of time to the firm's trade during the first year of assessment in which he is treated as carrying on that trade or in any of the following three years, he will again be restricted in the amount of any losses he can set off against income derived from non-partnership sources: Income and Corporation Taxes Act 1988, s.118ZE(1)–(4) (as added by the Finance Act 2004, s.124(1) and amended by the Finance Act 2005, s.72(3), Sch.11, Pt 2(4)), 118ZF (as added by *ibid.* and amended by the Finance Act 2005, s.78(2)). As in the last case, the restriction is framed by reference to the partner's contribution to the firm, including undrawn profits: *ibid.* s.118ZG (as added by *ibid.* and amended by the Finance Act 2005, s.72(5), 73(4), Sch.11, Pt 2(4)). In this case again the Partnerships (Restrictions on Contributions to a Trade) Regulations 2005, made pursuant to *ibid.* s.118ZN (as added by the Finance Act 2005, s.73(1)), apply and reference should be made to the summary set out *supra*, para.34–55. As to what amounts to a significant amount of time for this purpose, see the Income and Corporation Taxes Act 1988, s.118ZH(1) (as added by the Finance Act 2004, s.124(1)) and the Inland Revenue Press Release "Income tax: manipulation of partnership losses—examples" dated February 10, 2004, reproduced at [2004] S.T.I. 332. Where a non-active partner's contribution is reduced after relief has been given, any excess relief can be recovered from him by an additional charge to tax: Finance Act 2005, s.74. The above provisions do not apply to firms carrying on a profession.

Provision is made for the carry forward of losses that are not eligible to be set off against other income and these may become eligible for set off in future years if the partner's contribution increases (including a contribution on the partnership being wound up): Income and Corporation Taxes Act 1988, s.118ZI as added by the Finance Act 2004, s.124(1).

Film partnerships

A similar restriction on the use of losses applies to partners in a firm involved in the exploitation of films who do not devote a significant amount of time to that trade and are entitled to a guaranteed income: *ibid.* ss.118ZL, 118ZM, as added by the Finance Act 2004, s.125 and as respectively amended by the Income Tax (Trading and Other Income) Act 2005, Sch.1, paras 101, 102.   **34–55B**

An additional charge to tax may also be imposed where film-related losses have been relieved under the Income and Corporation Taxes Act 1988, ss.380, 381 (see *supra*, para.34–52) and a partner then disposes of his entitlement to profits in exchange for a non-taxable consideration or the amount of those losses subsequently exceeds his capital contribution (as defined): Finance Act 2004, ss.119 *et seq.* (as amended).

Exploitation of licences

Where relief in respect of "licence-related losses" has been or is to be claimed under the Income and Corporation Taxes Act 1988, ss.380, 381 (see *supra*, para.34–52), an additional charge to tax may be imposed on a non-active partner who disposes of a licence acquired in carrying on the firm's trade or any right to income thereunder in exchange for an non-taxable consideration: Finance Act 2004, ss.126 *et seq.*   **34–55C**

Terminal loss relief

NOTE 25. Now his "notional trade": see the Income Tax (Trading and Other Income) Act 2005, s.852(1), 4(a). As to the proposition in the latter part of the footnote, see *supra*, para.34–52, n.13.   **34–56**

NOTE 27. The Income and Corporation Taxes Act 1988, s.388(4) has been further amended by the Income Tax (Trading and Other Income) Act 2005, Sch.1, para.164(3), Sch.3.

NOTE 28. *ibid.* s.388(1) has been further amended by *ibid.* Sch.1, para.164(2), Sch.3.

NOTE 30. This is no longer a relevant concept.

34–57 NOTE 31. *ibid.* s.388(7) has been further amended by *ibid.* Sch.1, para.164(4).

NOTE 32. See *supra*, n.31.

Partnership business transferred to a company

34–58 NOTE 33. The Income and Corporation Taxes Act 1988, s.386(1) has been further amended by the Income Tax (Trading and Other Income) Act 2005, Sch.1, para.162, Sch.3.

6. PARTNERSHIPS WITH CORPORATE MEMBERS

34–59 It should be noted that the Income and Corporation Taxes Act 1988, s.111(1) (as amended by the Income Tax (Trading and Other Income) Act 2005, Sch.1, para.92(2)), which ensures that a partnership is not treated as an entity separate and distinct from the partners, continues to apply for corporation tax purposes, but its application to firms which do *not* carry on a trade or profession is by no means clear, with the repeal of *ibid.* s.111(6) by *ibid.* Sch.1, para.92(3), Sch.3. This appears to have been a legislative error (*cf. ibid.* s.114 as amended) and seems likely to be corrected in the near future.

Computation of partnership profits or losses

Stage 1—Partnership profits/losses

Debits or credits in relation to a money debt owed by or to the firm (or a loan relationship which would fall to be treated as such) are left out of account: Finance Act 1996, Sch.9, para.19(1), (2)(a), as added by the Finance Act 2002, Sch.25, para.25.

  The Inland Revenue is now HM Revenue & Customs: see the Commissioners for Revenue and Customs Act 2005, s.4.

NOTE 39. SP4/98 is now obsolete, since the position is now governed by the new legislation referred to in the text.

Stage 2—Corporate partner's profit share

34–60 At this stage any debits or credits in relation to a money debt owed by or to the firm (or a loan relationship which would fall to be treated as such) are brought into account and determined separately for each corporate partner: Finance Act

1996, Sch.9, para.19, as added by the Finance Act 2002, Sch.25, para.25 and amended by the Finance Act 2004, Sch.10, para.35, Sch.42, Pt 2(6) and the Income Tax (Trading and Other Income) Act 2005, Sch.1, paras 489(9) and prospectively further amended by the Finance (No.2) Act 2005, Sch.11, Pt 2(6). See also RI 248 ("Partnerships and loan relationships"), reproduced at [2003] S.T.I. 60.

NOTE 41. Note that this differs from the approach adopted in the Income Tax (Trading and Other Income) Act 2005, s.850, which, as noted *supra*, para.34–21, applies for income tax purposes even where some of the partners are not individuals.

NOTE 42. The Income and Corporation Taxes Act 1988, s.401(1) has been further amended by the Income Tax (Trading and Other Income) Act 2005, Sch.1, para.172.

NOTE 44. See now the Income Tax (Trading and Other Income) Act 2005, s.852.

Stage 3—Individual partner's profit share

NOTE 46. See now *ibid.* ss.849 *et seq.* And see further *supra*, para.34–21.　　**34–61**

Relief for losses

NOTE 48. It follows that the provisions of the Income and Corporation Taxes Act　**34–62** 1988, s.118ZN, as applied by *ibid.* s.117(5), (as amended), will *not* apply.

Anti-avoidance provisions

A further anti-avoidance provision has been introduced by the Finance Act 2004,　**34–63** s.131. This seeks to ensure that sums are not withdrawn from a partnership by a corporate partner *qua* capital or consideration for a disposal of all or part of its share which exceed the amount of its capital contribution and which actually represent profit in which it did not share by reason of an arrangement between the partners.

NOTE 51. The Income and Corporation Taxes Act 1988, s.116 has been further amended by the Income Tax (Trading and Other Income) Act 2005, Sch.1, para.96.

7. NON-RESIDENT AND DEEMED NON-RESIDENT PARTNERS

NOTE 53. See now, as to individuals, the Income Tax (Trading and Other Income)　**34–64** Act 2005, s.849(1), (2).

NOTE 55. See now *ibid.* s.858(1), (2).

Firms controlled in the United Kingdom

The Income Tax (Trading and Other Income) Act 2005, s.849(3) provides that　**34–65** where a partner is non-UK resident, the firm's profits and losses are calculated as if the firm were a non-UK resident individual, but it is no longer stated that such a partner's "notional trade" under *ibid.* s.852 is to be treated as if it were carried on in the UK. Nevertheless it is clear that such a partner will only be taxed on such part of his profit share as is derived from UK trading activities: *ibid.* s.4(2).

The position in relation to corporate partners is effectively unchanged.

NOTE 56. Note also *R. v. Holden* [2004] S.T.C. (SCD) 416, as to the effect of passing resolutions and signing documents consequent thereon.

NOTE 59. The Income and Corporation Taxes Act 1988, s.14(4) has been further amended by the Finance Act 2003, s.153(1)(a).

Firms controlled outside the United Kingdom

34–66 Where a firm is controlled and managed outside the UK and carries on a trade wholly or partly outside the UK, any UK resident individual partner who is either resident but not domiciled in the UK or not ordinarily resident in the UK and who makes a claim to that effect will have his share of the profits of the firm's trade arising in the UK ascertained and taxed in the normal way, but his share of profits arising outside the UK will be treated as relevant foreign income for the purposes of the Income Tax (Trading and Other Income) Act 2005, Pt 8 and will be charged on the remittance basis: *ibid.* s.857, applying the conditions set out in *ibid.* s.831.

Effect of a change in residence

34–67 This will now apply equally to that partner's "notional trade" and his "notional business".

NOTE 63. See now the Income Tax (Trading and Other Income) Act 2005, ss.852(6), 854(5). See further as to the expressions "notional trade" and "notional business", *supra*, paras 34–05, 34–06.

8. PAYMENTS TO OUTGOING PARTNERS AND THEIR DEPENDANTS

Consultancy agreements

34–68 NOTE 65. See now the Income Tax (Trading and Other Income) Act 2005, s.34(1)(a). Schs D and E have now respectively been replaced by the charge to tax under *ibid.* Pt 2 and the Income Tax (Earnings and Pensions) Act 2003, Pt 2.

NOTE 66. See *supra*, n.65.

34–69 NOTE 67. The Income and Corporation Taxes Act 1988, s.833(4)(c) has been further amended by the Income Tax (Trading and Other Income) Act 2005, Sch.1, para.338(3)(b).

Partnership annuities and other payments

NOTE 71. Note, however, the exceptional charges to tax on a non-taxable **34–70** payment which might be imposed in the situations considered *supra*, paras 34–55B, 34–55C.

NOTE 73. The first statutory reference should be to the Income and Corporation **34–71** Taxes Act 1988, s.347A(2)(c), which continues to apply. As to *ibid.* s.660A(9)(a), see now the Income Tax (Trading and Other Income) Act 2005, s.627(2)(a). The Income and Corporation Taxes Act 1988, s.125(3)(a) also continues to apply but has been amended by the Income Tax (Trading and Other Income) Act 2005, Sch.1, para.107(3).

NOTE 74. This should refer to the Income and Corporation Taxes Act 1988, s.347A(1).

NOTE 75. See now the Income Tax (Trading and Other Income) Act 2005, ss.624(1), 620(1). And see *supra*, para.34–12A.

NOTE 76. The Income and Corporation Taxes Act 1988, s.125(2) has been **34–72** amended by the Income Tax (Trading and Other Income) Act 2005, Sch.1, para.107(2) and the Finance Act 2005, s.91(2).

NOTE 77. *ibid.* 125(1) has been amended by the Finance (No.2) Act 2005, s.38(3), Sch.11, Pt 2(7).

Income and Corporation Taxes Act 1988, section 628

This section will, as from April 6, 2006, be repealed by the Finance Act 2004, **34–73** Sch.42, Pt 3.

NOTE 79. The Income and Corporation Taxes Act 1988, s.618 will also be repealed as from the same date by *ibid.*

NOTE 87. The second statutory reference should be to the Income and Corpora- **34–74** tion Taxes Act 1988, s.347A(2)(c). As to *ibid.* s.660A(9)(a), see now the Income Tax (Trading and Other Income) Act 2005, s.627(2)(a). The Income and Cor- poration Taxes Act 1988, s.125(3)(a) also continues to apply but has been amended by the Income Tax (Trading and Other Income) Act 2005, Sch.1, para.107(3).

Other arrangements

New legislation governing pension schemes is contained in the Finance Act 2004 **34–75** and will come into force on April 6, 2006.

NOTE 92. These sections will, as from April 6, 2006, be repealed by the Finance Act 2004, Sch.42, Pt 3.

NOTE 93. These sections will also, as from April 6, 2006, be repealed by *ibid.*

CHAPTER 35

CAPITAL GAINS TAX

1. INTRODUCTION

No special code for disposals of partnerships assets

35–01 The existing s.59 of the Taxation of Chargeable Gains Act 1992 has been designated as subs.(1) and the following additional subsections have been added by the Income Tax (Trading and Other Income) Act 2005, Sch.1, para.431:

"(2) Subsection (3) applies if—

(a) a person resident in the United Kingdom ("the resident partner") is a member of a partnership which resides outside the United Kingdom or which carries on any trade, profession or business the control and management of which is situated outside the United Kingdom, and

(b) by virtue of any arrangements falling within section 788 of the Taxes Act ("the arrangements") any of the capital gains of the partnership are relieved from capital gains tax in the United Kingdom.

(3) The arrangements do not affect any liability to capital gains tax in respect of the resident partner's share of any capital gains of the partnership."

35–02 NOTE 5. Statement of Practice D12 was reissued in a revised form on October 8, 2002 and in its current form (see *infra*, paras A6–04 *et seq.*) also applies to limited liability partnerships formed under the Limited Liability Partnerships Act 2000.

2. DISPOSALS OF PARTNERSHIP ASSETS OR OF SHARES THEREIN

A. DISPOSALS OF PARTNERSHIP ASSETS TO THIRD PARTIES

35–04 NOTE 8. The repeal of the Taxation of Chargeable Gains Act 1992, s.163(8) by the Finance Act 1998, s.140(2)(a), Sch.27, Pt III(31) has now had effect.

Reliefs available on disposal of partnership assets

(i) *"Roll-over" relief*

NOTE 19. An additional Class 7A, comprising payments under the income **35–07** support scheme for farmers, was inserted by the Finance Act 1993, section 86(2), (Single Payment Scheme) Order 2005 (SI 2005/409), art.2(2). As to the status of milk quota as a stand alone asset, note also *Foxton v. Revenue and Customs Commissioners* [2005] S.T.C. (SCD) 661.

NOTE 21. See also, as to this discretion, *R v. I.R.C.* [2004] S.T.C. 763.

(ii) *Retirement relief*

The complete phasing out of this relief and the repeal of the relevant statutory **35–09** provisions is now in effect.

(iii) *Taper relief*

In the case of business assets, full 75 per cent relief is now obtained after only **35–10** two years: Taxation of Chargeable Gains Act 1992, s.2A(5), as amended by the Finance Act 2002, s.46.

As to the treatment of a share of goodwill acquired in stages for the purposes of taper relief, see *infra*, para.35–37.

NOTE 29. The Taxation of Chargeable Gains Act 1992, Sch.A1, para.5 has been substituted by the Finance Act 2003, s.160(3). And note *Patel v. Maidment* [2004] S.T.C. (S.C.D.) 41.

NOTE 30. See now Ray, *Partnership Taxation*, para.14–92.

NOTE 34. See now the Taxation of Chargeable Gains Act 1992, Sch.A1, para.5 (1A)(a), as substituted by the Finance Act 2003, s.160(3). Similarly where the partnership comprises a company which is, as regards that partner, a "qualifying company": *ibid.* paras 5(1B)(c) (as substituted by *ibid.*), 6 (as amended).

NOTE 36. See the text above. As noted, under the amended provision 50 per cent relief is achieved after the first year.

NOTE 39. The Taxation of Chargeable Gains Act 1992, s.2A(8) has been further amended by the Finance Act 2002, Sch.40, Pt 3(2).

NOTE 41. Now only two years in the case of a business asset: see the text above.

NOTE 42. The Taxation of Chargeable Gains Act 1992, Sch.A1, para.15 has been further amended by the Finance Act 2003, s.160(4)(b).

35–11 (iv) *"Hold-over" relief*

Retirement relief has now been wholly phased out.

NOTE 47. See the text, *supra*.

NOTE 51. The Taxation of Chargeable Gains Act 1992, s.2A has been further amended by the Finance Act 2002, s.46, Sch.40, Pt 3(3).

B. DISPOSAL OF PARTNERSHIP SHARES

The general treatment of dealings between partners

35–12 NOTE 53. And note also *Mansworth v. Jelley* [2003] S.T.C. 53, CA (although the effect of this decision was reversed by the Taxation of Chargeable Gains Act 1992, s.144ZA, as added by the Finance Act 2003, s.158(1) and amended by the Finance (No.2) Act 2005, Sch.5, para.1).

35–13 NOTE 60. And see *Mansworth v. Jelley, supra*.

NOTE 63. The Taxation of Chargeable Gains Act 1992, s.2A has been further amended by the Finance Act 2002, s.46, Sch.40, Pt 3(3).

Revenue practice: rearrangement of shares without payment

35–14 NOTE 67. The Taxation of Chargeable Gains Act 1992, s.2A has been further amended by the Finance Act 2002, s.46, Sch.40, Pt 3(3).

Revenue practice: rearrangement of shares coupled with a payment

35–16 NOTE 72. The Taxation of Chargeable Gains Act 1992, s.2A has been further amended by the Finance Act 2002, s.46, Sch.40, Pt 3(3).

Revenue practice: revaluation of partnership shares

35–18 NOTE 80. The Taxation of Chargeable Gains Act 1992, s.2A has been further amended by the Finance Act 2002, s.46, Sch.40, Pt 3(3).

NOTE 81. *ibid.* s.4(2) has been further amended by the Income Tax (Trading and Other Income) Act 2005, Sch.1, para.427.

Entire disposal of partnership share

35–19 NOTE 86. See *supra*, n.80.

Resident partner in non-resident firm

35–21A Where a firm which is non-resident or the business of which is controlled and managed outside the UK realises a gain, a UK resident partner in that firm will not be able to avail himself of any double tax treaty relief which would otherwise apply to the firm's capital gains in order to frank his share of that gain: Taxation of Chargeable Gains Act 1992, s.59(2), (3) (as added by the Income Tax (Trading and Other Income) Act 2005, Sch.1, para.431), reproduced *supra*, para.35–01.

Relief available on retirement of partner

This relief has now been entirely phased out and the relevant sections repealed. **35–22 to 35–24**

Mergers and "roll-over" relief

NOTE 22. The Taxation of Chargeable Gains Act 1992, s.2A has been further amended by the Finance Act 2002, s.46, Sch.40, Pt 3(3). **35–29**

C. DISTRIBUTION OF PARTNERSHIP ASSETS AMONGST PARTNERS

NOTE 31. The Taxation of Chargeable Gains Act 1992, s.2A has been further amended by the Finance Act 2002, s.46, Sch.40, Pt 3(3). **35–31**

3. ADMINISTRATION AND COMPUTATION

Computation of gains

(a) Partnership shares acquired in stages

It is now clear that HM Revenue & Customs will regard goodwill which is self-generated and which does not appear in the firm's balance sheet as a non-fungible asset which will not therefore constitute "securities" for the purposes of the Taxation of Chargeable Gains Act 1992, s.104(3): Statement of Practice D12, para.12, *infra*, para.A6–16. Similarly in the case of *acquired* goodwill which is not reflected in its balance sheet at a value exceeding cost, although such goodwill will be treated as an asset separate and distinct from any self-generated goodwill: *ibid.* **35–37**

NOTE 48. See now Ray, *Partnership Taxation*, paras 14.102 *et seq.*

NOTE 49. See now *ibid.* para.14.105.

NOTE 50. The Taxation of Chargeable Gains Act 1992, s.2A has been further amended by the Finance Act 2002, s.46, Sch.40, Pt 3(3).

NOTE 52. See the text, *supra*.

NOTE 57. The view formerly expressed in Ray, *Partnership Taxation* at para.14.174 has not been retained.

(b) Shares held as partnership assets

NOTE 60. And see *supra*, para.35–37. **35–38**

INHERITANCE TAX

2. EXEMPTIONS AND RELIEFS

Dispositions allowable for income tax

36–12 NOTE 41. The Inheritance Tax Act 1984, s.12(2) is prospectively amended by the Finance Act 2004, s.203(2).

Agricultural property relief

36–13 NOTE 45. Note *Rosser v. I.R.C.* [2003] S.T.C. (SCD) 311.

36–14 Note that where land has been transferred from one partner to another, continued use of that land by the partnership may attract a charge to *income* tax on the transferor partner, under the pre-owned assets regime, unless it amounts to a gift with a reservation: see *supra*, paras 34–30A and *infra*, paras 36–40 *et seq.*

Business relief

36–16 NOTE 66. See also *I.R.C. v. George* [2004] S.T.C. 147, CA.

3. CHARGEABLE TRANSFERS

A. FORMATION OF A PARTNERSHIP

Capital and capital profits

36–26 NOTE 6. If the "look through" argument were to succeed and there was held to be a gift with a reservation in relation to land or a chattel, there would be no scope for a charge to income tax under the pre-owned assets regime noticed *supra*, para.34–30A.

Partnership assurance schemes

Note that HM Revenue & Customs have also confirmed that such a scheme will **36–37** not, in general, fall within the pre-owned assets regime for income tax purposes: see *supra*, para.34–30B.

Property of a partner used by the firm

NOTE 51. Note that the Finance Act 1986, s.102 has, as regards transfers between **36–38** spouses, been amended by the Finance Act 2003, s.185, thus *prima facie* reversing the decision in *I.R.C. v. Eversden* [2003] S.T.C. 822, CA. But see further Foster, *Inheritance Tax*, para.C4.31, as to the effects of this amendment.

Reservation of benefit

Interest in land

If no reservation of benefit arises in such a case, the transferor partner *may* be **36–41** subject to an income tax charge under the Finance Act 2004, Sch.15 (pre-owned assets), unless he actively opts in to the reservation of benefit regime under *ibid.* Sch.15, para.21. See further *supra*, para.34–30A.

Section 102

NOTE 58. And note also *I.R.C. v. Eversden* [2002] S.T.C. 1109, although the final **36–42** part of the decision no longer applies in the face of the amendments to the Finance Act 1986, s.102 introduced by the Finance Act 2003, s.185. Only the spouse exemption issue was pursued on the appeal at [2003] S.T.C. 822. See also *supra*, para.36–38, n.51.

NOTE 59. Equally, there will be no income tax charge under the pre-owned assets regime in such a case: see *supra*, para.34–30A.

Section 102A

NOTE 70. Again, there will be no income tax charge under the pre-owned assets **36–43** regime in this case: see *supra*, para.34–30A.

Undivided share of an interest in land

NOTE 76. There may, however, be an income tax charge under the pre-owned **36–44** assets regime: see *supra*, para.34–30A.

Assets other than land

In the case of a chattel, an income tax charge under the pre-owned assets regime **36–45** may arise if there is no reservation of benefit: see *supra*, paras 34–30A. A similar charge may also be imposed in the case of intangible property, but only if it is comprised in a settlement: see *supra*, para.34–30B.

B. CONTINUATION OF A PARTNERSHIP

36–50   NOTE 92. Note also, in this context, the potential application of the pre-owned assets regime: see *supra*, paras 34–30A, 34–30B, 36–41, 36–45.

5. VALUATION AND ADMINSTRATION

Valuation of goodwill

36–71   NOTE 72. The National Health Service Act 1977, s.54 has been further amended by the Health and Social Care (Community Health and Standards) Act 2003, Sch.11, para.26 and *ibid.* Sch.10 has been further amended by *ibid.* Sch.11, para.43. A further prohibition on the sale of goodwill by various types of contractors and certain medical practitioners providing "essential services" is also to be found in the Primary Medical Services (Sale of Goodwill and Restrictions on Sub-contracting) Regulations 2004 (SI 2004/906), reg.3(1).

CHAPTER 37

VALUE ADDED TAX

1. REGISTRATION

NOTE 2. In *Berwick v. Customs & Excise Commissioners*, May 31, 2002 (Lawtel   **37–01**
18/7/02), the Valued Added Tax Tribunal ordered the compulsory deregistration
of a partnership purporting to carry on the business of yacht chartering on the
grounds that it was not carrying on any economic activity within the meaning of
Art.4 of the Sixth Directive (*i.e.* EC Council Directive 77/388). The decision is
strikingly similar to that in *Three H. Aircraft Hire v. Customs & Excise Commissioners*. See further, as to this test, *Customs & Excise Commissioners v. Yarburgh
Children's Trust* [2002] S.T.C. 207; *Customs & Excise Commissioners v. St.
Paul's Community Project Ltd* [2005] S.T.C. 95; *Finanzamt Offenbach am Main-
Land v. Faxworld Vorgründungsgesellschaft etc.* [2005] S.T.C. 1192, ECJ. And
note also, as to the status of dealings between a partner and his own partnership,
Staatsecretaris van Financiën v. Heerma [2001] S.T.C. 1437, ECJ.

Taxable supplies in the United Kingdom

NOTE 5. See now the Value Added Tax (Increase of Registration Limits) Order   **37–02**
2005 (SI 2005/727), art.2(a). The limit is currently £60,000. And note, as to the
position following a transfer as a going concern, the decision of the VAT Tribunal
in *Ludovico v. Customs & Excise Commissioners*, May 24, 2004 (Lawtel
28/6/04).

NOTE 6. See now *ibid.* Again the prescribed amount is currently £60,000.

NOTE 8. See now *ibid.* art.2(b). The prescribed amount is currently £58,000.

Acquisitions from other E.C. states

NOTE 20. See now the Value Added Tax (Increase of Registration Limits) Order   **37–04**
2005, art.3(a). The prescribed amount is currently £60,000.

NOTE 21. See now *ibid.*

Notification and registration

37–06 Note 28. This footnote should refer to the Value Added Tax Act 1994, Sch.2 rather than Sch.2A.

Registration of partnerships

37–07 See also, as to the effect of the Value Added Tax Act 1994, s.45, HM Revenue & Customs' Business Brief 21/04 "VAT—VAT position of share issues and partnership contributions following the ECJ decision in *KapHag Renditefonds*" issued on August 10, 2004, *infra*, para.A6–33.

Note 30. Note also *Ali v. Customs & Excise Commissioners* [2004] S.T.I. 1302, where the daughter was held to be a partner. A joint venture may well not constitute a partnership: see *Thorstone Developments Ltd v. Commissioners of Customs & Excise*, October 14, 2002 (VAT Trib., NLC 702107202); also para.5–07.

Attempts to avoid registration

37–11 Note 53. An attempt to invoke the Value Added Tax Act 1994, Sch.1, para.1A failed in *Trippitt v. Customs & Excise Commissioners* [2002] S.T.I. 214. Note also *Turner v. HMRC* [2005] S.T.I. 1446, where the attempt failed because the directions under that paragraph were incorrectly issued. In *Skelton Waste Disposal v. Customs & Excise Commissioners* [2002] S.T.I. 215 and *Barton v. Customs & Excise Commissioners* [2003] S.T.I. 1583, the Commissioners again sought to argue that there was in substance a single partnership.

Note 54. Note that all statutory restrictions on the size of partnerships were removed by the Regulatory Reform (Reform of 20 Member Limit in Partnerships etc.) Order 2002 (SI 2002/3203), reg.2, with effect from December 21, 2002.

Changes in the firm

37–13 Note 62. See now HM Revenue & Customs Notice 700, paras 26.2, 26.3.

Cancellation of registration

37–14 Note 65. *Registration pursuant to the Value Added Tax Act 1984, Sched. 1*: See now the Value Added Tax (Increase of Registration Limits) Order 2005, art.2(b). The limit is currently £58,000. *Registration pursuant to ibid. Sched. 3*: See now the Value Added Tax (Increase of Registration Limits) Order 2005, art.3(b). The limit is currently £60,000.

Note 67. *Berwick v. Customs & Excise Commissioners*, May 31, 2002 (Lawtel 18/7/02), noticed *supra*, para.37–01, n.2, is a recent example of a case within this class.

2. TAXABLE SUPPLIES

NOTE 71. See also *Birketts v. Customs & Excise Commissioners* [2002] S.T.I. **37–15**
371; *Oglethorpe Sturton & Gillibrand v. Customs & Excise Commissioners*
[2002] S.T.I. 834.

Offices held by partners

NOTE 75. *Cf. Bray Walker v. Customs & Excise Commissioners* [2004] S.T.I. 575, **37–16**
where the partner was a director and could not be shown to be acting as an
employee.

There nevertheless appears to be some evidence of a hardening of attitude on the **37–17**
part of what is now HM Revenue & Customs regarding offices and appointments
held by partners (albeit with no great success), as witness the following decisions
of the VAT Tribunal (all of which concerned offices held by partners in firms of
solicitors): *Birketts v. Customs & Excise Commissioners, supra*; *Oglethorpe
Sturton & Gillibrand v. Customs & Excise Commissioners, supra*; *Bray Walker
v. Customs & Excise Commissioners, supra*.

Use of partnership property by the partners

NOTE 91. The attitude of HM Revenue & Customs to the potential charge on the **37–19**
transfer of a partnership share has now been clarified: see *infra*, paras 37–25 to
37–29.

Sale of partnership assets

Goods

This can include the case where one or more partners withdraw assets from the **37–20**
firm: *Fengate Developments v. Customs & Excise Commissioners* [2005] S.T.C.
191, CA. There the asset transferred was land in respect of which the partnership
had elected to waive exemption. Other circumstances in which a charge to value
added tax may be incurred on the withdrawal of assets are considered in the
Business Brief 21/04 "VAT—VAT position of share issues and partnership
contributions following the ECJ decision in *KapHag Renditefonds*" dated August
10, 2004, section 1, para.B(vii), reproduced *infra*, para.A6–32.

NOTE 94. The Value Added Tax Act 1994, Sch.4, para.5(2)(a) was substituted by
the Finance Act 2003, s.21(2). This amendment superseded the Value Added Tax
(Business Gifts of Small Value) Order 2001. See also the Value Added Tax Act
1994, Sch.4, para.5(2ZA) as added by the Finance Act 2003, s.21(3).

Sale of partnership business as a going concern

NOTE 4. The Value Added Tax (Special Provisions) Order 1995, art.5(2) has been **37–22**
amended and *ibid.* art.5(2A), (2B) added by the Value Added Tax (Special
Provisions) (Amendment) Order 2004 (SI 2004/779), arts 3, 4. And note, as to

what may amount to a sale as a going concern, the decision of the VAT Tribunal in *International Supplier Auditing Ltd v. Customs & Excise Commissioners* [2003] S.T.I. 1512 (sale of assets at a time when no business was being carried on); also *Ludovico v. Customs & Excise Commissioners*, May 24, 2004 (Lawtel 28/6/04).

NOTE 5. See now the amendments to the Value Added Tax Act 1994, Sch.1, paras 1(2), (3) introduced by the Value Added Tax (Increase of Registration Limits) Order 2005 (SI 2005/727), art.2. The Value Added Tax Regulations 1995, reg.6 has been further amended by the Value Added Tax (Amendment) (No.3) Regulations 2004 (SI 2004/1675), reg.3.

Partnership ceasing to be a taxable person

37–23   NOTE 9. The Value Added Tax Regulations 1995, reg.9(3) has been amended by the Enterprise Act (Insolvency) Order 2003 (SI 2003/2096), Sch., Pt II, para.56.

Dissolution of the partnership

37–24   NOTE 14a. And note the decision in *Fengate Developments v. Customs & Excise Commissioners* [2005] S.T.C. 191, CA, noticed *supra*, para.37–20 (albeit that there the supply was not made on dissolution).

Transfers of partnership shares

37–25 to
37–29   Following the decision of the European Court of Justice in *KapHag Renditefonds v. Finanzamt Charlottenberg* (Case C-442/01), it is now clear that the mere contribution of capital on admission to a partnership does not of itself involve a taxable supply on the basis that there is a reciprocal supply by the partnership, although there are clearly circumstances in which there *may* be a taxable supply for other reasons: see the Business Brief 21/04 "VAT—VAT position of share issues and partnership contributions following the ECJ decision in *KapHag Renditefonds*" dated August 10, 2004, s.1, para.B(i)–(iii), *infra*, paras A6–26 *et seq*. In an appropriate case, any such supply may be eligible to be treated as a transfer of a going concern: see *ibid.* para.B(iv), *infra*, para.A6–29.

In consequence of the above ruling, on November 19, 2004 HM Customs & Excise (as it then was) issued a further Business Brief (30/04) "VAT and partnership 'shares'" (reproduced *infra*, paras A6–34 *et seq*.), the content of which is by no means on all fours with the analysis in the existing text. The following propositions are derived from that Business Brief:

(i) A partnership share comprises services *not* goods. This reflects the analysis in the latter part of para.37–28, based on the decision in *Border Flying Co v. The Commissioners*.

(ii) A disposal of a share for no consideration will not constitute a supply.

(iii) A disposal of a share which was originally acquired by a partner for investment purposes (*i.e.* he was intending to be a sleeping or limited partner) will not constitute a supply, even if made for a consideration, because no economic activity on his part is involved on that disposal.

(iv) Where, however, the share was originally acquired by a partner who was a taxable person in his own right *and* in the course or furtherance of his own existing economic activities, its disposal for a consideration is likely to involve a supply. The position is *a fortiori* where that partner's business is trading in partnership shares. This to an extent mirrors the analysis in para.37–29.

(v) Equally, where the share was originally acquired by a partner who was a taxable person in his own right and with a view to undertaking an active role in the partnership, its disposal for a consideration may also involve a supply. This again mirrors the analysis in para.37–29.

(vi) The Value Added Tax Act 1994, s.45(1) will not be regarded as applying in any such case so as to negate the existence of a supply. This is directly contrary to the arguments canvassed in para.37–26 and reflects the view of HM Revenue & Customs as to the effect of that section: see also Business Brief 21/04, *infra*, para.A6–33.

(vii) Significantly, a supply which is treated as made in any of the above ways will be an exempt financial service within the Value Added Tax Act 1994, Sch.9, Group 5, so that no tax will be chargeable. This will obviously have an impact on the deductibility of any input tax. Whether the supply could also be ignored as a transfer of a going concern and thus within the Value Added Tax (Special Provisions) Order 1995 (see para.37–22) is, perhaps, largely academic.

3. ADMINISTRATION

Notification by partners

NOTE 36. See also the Value Added Tax Act 1994, Sch.3A, para.8, as added by the Finance Act 2000, Sch.36. **37–31**

Failure to notify change in firm

NOTE 41. See *Jamieson v. Customs & Excise Commissioners* [2002] S.T.C. 1418; also *Hussein v. Customs & Excise Commissioners* [2003] V. & D.R. 439; *Miah v Customs & Excise Commissioners* [2004] S.T.I. 449. In all of these cases the partnership had been dissolved. **37–32**

Liability for tax

NOTE 49. See now *Jamieson v. Customs & Excise Commissioners* [2002] S.T.C. 1418; also the other cases cited *supra*, para.37–32, n.41. **37–35**

Penalty assessments

NOTE 51. See also *Islam v. Customs & Excise Commissioners (No.17834)*, July 25, 2002. *Cf. Segger v. Customs & Excise Commissioners*, June 29, 2004 (Lawtel 9/9/04), where the wife's involvement as a partner was not admitted. **37–56**

CHAPTER 38

STAMP DUTY

2. STAMP DUTY LAND TAX

Introduction

38–12   In the case of a partnership owning land or an interest in land, most transactions of the type considered in this Chapter will now at least be potentially subject to a charge to stamp duty land tax (SDLT), which was first introduced by the Finance Act 2003, Pt 4, but only applied to partnerships by amendments contained in the Finance Act 2004, Sch.41. Initially, such transactions were excluded from the charge: Finance Act 2003, Sch.15, para.9(1) in its original form.

SDLT is only chargeable in respect of a "chargeable interest" as defined in the Finance Act 2003, s.48(1), *i.e.* an estate, interest, right or power in or over land in the United Kingdom or the benefit of an obligation, restriction or condition affecting the value of any such estate, interest, right or power. This clearly includes a lease, although a tenancy at will or a *licence* to use or occupy land is an exempt interest and thus outwith the scope of SDLT (*ibid.* s.48(2)(a), (c)(i)), but there may ultimately be a charge if the tenant/licensee is given a power to direct or request that the land be conveyed to a third party or to himself and that contract is substantially performed: *ibid.* s.44A, as added by the Finance Act 2004, Sch.39, para.4(1). It should be emphasised that, unlike stamp duty, a charge to SDLT is *not* dependent on the existence or otherwise of any document evidencing a land transaction.

In what follows, all references to Sch.15 to the Finance Act 2003 are to that Schedule as amended by the Finance Act 2004, Sch.41, para.1, although later amendments are specifically noted where relevant.

Residual stamp duty charge

38–13   It should be noted that the charge to stamp duty was abolished save in relation to instruments relating to stock or marketable securities: Finance Act 2003, s.125(1). Special provision is made to avoid a double charge to duty in the case of transfers of a share in a partnership which holds, *inter alia*, a chargeable interest and stocks or other marketable securities: *ibid.* Sch.15, paras 32, 33, as amended, in the case of the latter section, by the Finance (No.2) Act 2005, Sch.10, para.21(2). It was originally not clear whether the pre-existing stamp duty regime still applied to such transfers in other cases, given the terms of the Finance Act 2003, Sch.15, para.31(1), (2), which appeared to preserve the old

[154]

regime in *all* cases. Now, however, the doubt would appear to have been resolved by *ibid.* Sch.15, para.33(1), (1A) (as substituted by the Finance (No.2) Act 2005, Sch.10, para.21(2)), which is of general application, although an adjudication stamp may still be required in such a case under the Stamp Act 1891, s.12: see *ibid.* Sch.15, para.33(1A), (8).

Transactions with third parties

Where a partnership acquires a chargeable interest from a third party (*i.e.* what **38–14** is styled an "ordinary partnership transaction": see *ibid.* Sch.15, para.5), SDLT will be chargeable on normal principles. The partners at the date of the relevant transaction and any partner who joins the firm thereafter will be responsible for submitting a land transaction return and complying with the other obligations imposed on a purchaser but only the former will be jointly and severally liable for any tax due: *ibid.* Sch.15, paras 6, 7. However, a majority of the partners may appoint one or more representative partners to fulfil their obligations, on giving notice to HM Revenue & Customs: *ibid.* Sch.15, para.8.

Scope and operation of SDLT charge on partnership transactions

The new SDLT regime imposed in the case of transactions of the type specified **38–15** in the Finance Act 2003, Sch.15, para.9(1) applies to all partnerships within the meaning of the Partnership Act 1890, as well as limited partnerships registered under the Limited Partnerships Act 1907 and limited liability partnerships formed under the Limited Liability Partnerships Act 2000: *ibid.* Sch.15, para.1. Partnerships or limited liability partnerships formed under the laws of another jurisdiction are also within the ambit of SDLT, irrespective of whether they enjoy separate legal personality: *ibid.* Sch.15, paras 1, 2. It follows that all partnerships are regarded as transparent for SDLT purposes, even though it is provided that a partnership has continuity notwithstanding a change in its membership: *ibid.* Sch.15, para.3.

For the purposes of SDLT, a chargeable asset will be regarded as partnership property where it is "held by or on behalf of a partnership, *or the members of a partnership*, for the purposes of the partnership business" (emphasis supplied): *ibid.* Sch.15, para.34(1). This appears artificially to extend the scope of partnership property to include an asset held by one or more partners *outside* the partnership, if they nevertheless hold it for the purposes of its business; *sed quaere.* This may represent a trap for the unwary, particularly on the subsequent dissolution of the partnership: see *infra*, para.38–21.

Where the size of a partner's share falls to be determined, regard is had only to his share of *income* profits, even though profits attributable to the chargeable asset in question may fall to be divided in some other way, *i.e.* in specified capital profit or asset surplus shares: see *ibid.* Sch.15, para.34(2). This approach is inexplicable (and logically insupportable) and, moreover, departs from the approach adopted for the purposes of capital gains tax: see, *supra*, para.35–05. It also appears wholly to ignore the existence of "salaried" or "fixed share" partners, who may have no entitlement whatsoever to share in the capital assets or profits of the firm and whose share of income profits may be limited to a fixed sum. It follows that, whilst the approach adopted in the legislation militates in

STAMP DUTY

favour of all profits being shared in the same way, in order to avoid anomalous results in those cases where an SDLT charge is likely to be incurred, this will not be possible in all cases. Equally, it would seem that a change in the partners' capital profit or asset sharing ratios will not *per se* have any impact for SDLT purposes.

It should be noted that, whilst the definition of "connected persons" in the Income and Corporation Taxes Act 1988, s.839 is applied for SDLT purposes, partners will only be treated as connected *otherwise* than through their relationship as partners: Finance Act 2003, Sch.15, para.39. It follows that, in the vast majority of cases, the connected persons rules will not apply.

Chargeable partnership transactions

38–16 The impact of SDLT can most conveniently be considered in the context of the four stages in the life of a partnership listed in para.38–03. There is, however, a blanket exemption for all *acquisitions* of partnership shares which do not fall within one of three specified charging provisions: *ibid.* Sch.15, para.29.

(1) *Formation of a Partnership*

Where an incoming partner transfers a chargeable interest to a partnership on or after its formation otherwise than in return for an actual consideration, SDLT will be charged by reference to a proportion of the market value of that interest: *ibid.* Sch.15, para.10(1)–(3). The relevant proportion will, in essence, be that which is *not* retained by the incoming partner and any partner(s) with whom he is connected otherwise than in that capacity, but the computation is a complex one and is dependent on identifying "the sum of the lower proportions": *ibid.* Sch.15, para.12(1). This five step process involves ascertaining the lower of

    (a) the total of the interest held by the incoming partner *prior* to the transfer apportioned between himself and any partner(s) with whom he is connected; and

    (b) the partnership shares of the incoming partner and any partner(s) with whom he is connected immediately *after* the transfer.

This sum is then deducted from 100 and what remains, when expressed as a percentage, is the proportion of the market value treated as disposed of and thus chargeable to SDLT. Thus, where an incoming partner, A, contributes land to an equal partnership between himself and B, with whom he is not connected, he will, predictably, be regarded as having disposed of the land for a consideration equal to one-half of its then market value. Were A and B connected persons otherwise than as partners, then the land would still, in effect, be regarded as within A's ownership and no consideration would be deemed to arise. The position would be the same if a third party, C, connected with both A and B transferred the land to the partnership for no consideration. If both A and B contribute land to the partnership, the same computation will have to be carried out in respect of each transfer. Clearly, in the case of a larger partnership, the computation process will be more complex. Any joint tenancy which may exist

[156]

in the land prior to the transfer is ignored and treated as if it were a tenancy in common in equal shares: *ibid.* Sch.15, para.12(2).

Where consideration for the transfer is provided by the firm, then SDLT is chargeable on a proportion of the consideration *in addition* to the proportion of the market value treated as disposed of: *ibid.* Sch.15, paras 10(2), (4). In this instance, the relevant proportion is "the sum of the lower proportions" (see, *supra*) expressed as a percentage: *ibid.* Sch.15, para.10(4). However, special rules apply where the chargeable consideration consists of or includes rent: see *ibid.* Sch.15, para.11, applying *ibid.* Sch.5 with amendments.

It should be noted that the above regime appears to apply not only where land is transferred *into* a partnership, but also where a chargeable interest, such as a right of occupation, becomes partnership property: see *supra*, para.38–15. This presupposes that either the owner of the land is (or becomes) a partner or is connected to a partner, otherwise SDLT would be chargeable (if at all) on normal principles. In such a case, a preferential share of profits receivable by a partner in lieu of a formal rent would clearly constitute consideration for the transfer, but if the only interest acquired by the firm were a tenancy at will or a licence, no SDLT would be chargeable in any event: see *supra*, para.38–12.

Special rules apply where such a transfer is, within 3 years, followed by a withdrawal of capital, etc., from the firm: see *infra*, para.38–18. Special rules also apply in the case of a transfer of land to a corporate partnership where *all* the partners are bodies corporate and "the sum of the lower proportions" is 75 or more, so that group relief would be available: *ibid.* Sch.15, para.13.

(2) *Alteration of Partners' Shares, etc.*

The key issues in determining whether such an alteration is a chargeable transac- **38–17** tion are whether (a) it involves a transfer of the whole or any part of a share in a partnership which holds a chargeable interest as "relevant partnership prop- erty" and (b) the partner(s) acquiring any part of that share gave consideration in money or money's worth therefor: see the Finance Act 2003, Sch.15, paras 14(1), (4)(a), (5), 36(a). As regards condition (a), land transferred to the partnership in connection with the transfer of the share is ignored: *ibid.* Sch.15, para.15(5)(a). If either condition is not satisfied, no SDLT is chargeable. Moreover, a lease at a market rent and granted otherwise than for a premium is not, in general, regarded as "relevant partnership property", provided that, if the term is for more than five years, the rent is reviewed to a market rent every five years: *ibid.* Sch.15, para.15. It should, however, be noted that an upwards only rent review would appear not to qualify for this purpose, since it, by definition, cannot be guaranteed that, following the review, a market rent will be payable.

The fact that the share transferred does not carry any direct or indirect right to share in the chargeable interest held by the firm does not appear to matter: see *ibid.* Sch.15, para.14(1)(c), (5). This is, perhaps, consistent with the fact that regard is for SDLT purposes only had to the income profit sharing ratios: see, *supra*, para.38–15. It would seem to follow that an increase (or reduction) in the fixed share of profits of a salaried or fixed share partner will potentially be regarded as a transfer of a share in the partnership for this purpose. Indeed, assuming that the firm's profits do not remain static, there will almost inevitably be a variation in such a partner's share, expressed as a proportion of the whole profits, year on year.

Condition (b) above, *i.e.* whether consideration in money or money's worth has been received, is thus critical. In the type of case cited in the last paragraph, the payment of consideration is most unlikely. Even in the case of an equity partner whose share increases, it is submitted that consideration cannot properly be found in his assumption of a greater share of the partnership liabilities save, perhaps, where there is a partnership debt secured on the land (*ibid.* Sch.4, para.8(1A), as added by the Finance Act 2004, s.301(3)); *sed quaere.* Withdrawal of money from the partnership by a partner whose share reduces is more problematic, even where the sum withdrawn constitutes a balance otherwise due to him. Thus, the legislation provides that a partner who transfers the whole or part of his share to an incoming partner and who, pursuant to any "arrangements" entered into at the time, then or thereafter withdraws money from the firm will in all cases be treated as having received consideration in money or money's worth: *ibid.* Sch.15, paras 14(4)(b), 36(b). For this purpose arrangements include "any scheme, agreement or understanding, whether or not legally enforceable": *ibid.* Sch.15, para.40. The withdrawal of any capital or current account balances would appear to suffice for this purpose, since the legislation does not state by whom or in what circumstances the payment must have been made. If, however, it can be shown that the withdrawal was wholly unconnected to the transfer and/ or that it was not in contemplation at the time it was made, no charge will be imposed, unless consideration in money or money's worth is given in some other manner. The position where there is a transfer or accruer of a share as between *continuing* partners, whether accompanied or followed by a withdrawal of money, is less clear. From the way in which the legislation is framed, it would appear that no consideration will be regarded as given even where the withdrawal is in pursuance of contemporary "arrangements" (*cf. ibid.* Sch.15, paras 14(4)(a), (b), 36(a) and (b)), but this would, undoubtedly, be a curiously inconsistent result. See further, *infra*, para.38–19.

38–18   In cases where an alteration of the partners' shares does involve a chargeable transaction, the SDLT charge will be by reference to a proportion of the market value of the relevant chargeable interest equal to the increase in the acquiring partner's share of the firm's income profits: see the Finance Act 2003 Sch.15, paras 14(6), (7)(b), 34(2) and *supra*, para.38–15. It would seem to follow that a transfer of a share in *capital* profits for a consideration would not involve an SDLT charge, even though it would clearly carry a right to a share in the proceeds of the land owned by the firm. In the rare case where the consideration takes the form of a transfer of land owned by a partner, the rules governing exchanges in *ibid.* Sch.4, para.5 will apply: *ibid.* Sch.15, para.16(1). The partition rules (*ibid.* Sch.4, para.6) will, in such a case, be excluded: *ibid.* Sch.15, para.16(3).

Anti-avoidance provisions apply where a partnership share is transferred pursuant to "arrangements" put in place when the land in question was originally transferred to the partnership: *ibid.* Sch.15, para.17. In such a case, the subsequent transfer will be chargeable even if no consideration is received therefor. This will seemingly cover any arrangements under the partnership agreement, *e.g.* for changes in the income profit sharing ratios pursuant to a "lockstep" or similar arrangement or even for the payment of the entitlement of an outgoing partner, provided that the subsequent transfer is made by the partner who originally transferred the land to the firm. As previously noted, special rules also apply in those cases where both stamp duty and SDLT would potentially be chargeable: see *ibid.* Sch.15, paras 32, 33.

The above anti-avoidance provision has now been supplemented by an automatic charge imposed on the partners in a firm when a transfer of a chargeable interest to the firm is followed within three years by the transferor partner withdrawing money or money's worth, otherwise than in the form of income profits, by way of a return of capital, a reduction in his share, retirement terms or a direct or indirect repayment of the whole or any part of a loan previously made to the firm: see *ibid.* Sch.15, para.17A(1)–(3), (5) (as added by the Finance (No.2) Act 2005, Sch.10, para.10). Such a "qualifying event" is treated as a land transaction which is chargeable (*ibid.* Sch.15, para.17A(4)) and the consideration is the amount withdrawn or repaid, but may not, in the case of a loan, exceed the amount of that loan or, in any case, the market value of the chargeable interest at the date of the original transfer to the firm reduced by any amount previously charged to tax (*ibid.* Sch.15, para.17A(7)). It would seem that the partner receiving the consideration is deemed to be a purchaser for this purpose: *ibid.* Sch.15, para.17A(5). Whether this is still the case if he has retired from the firm is not entirely clear.

It should be noted that transfers of partnership shares are not notifiable if the relevant consideration does not exceed the zero rate threshold, *i.e.* £150,000 (assuming that the firm does not own residential land): *ibid.* s.55, Sch.15, para.30.

(2) *Retirement and Admission of Partners*

Outgoing partners

The position in the case of a retirement, etc., is broadly similar to that which **38–19** applies on an alteration in partnership shares, particularly where there are "arrangements" under which the retiring partner transfers his share to an incoming partner and withdraws money or money's worth from the firm (see the Finance Act 2003, Sch.15, paras 14(4)(b), 36(b) and *supra*, para.38–17) or where he has retired within three years of making a chargeable transfer to the firm (see *ibid.* Sch.15, para.17A, as added by the Finance (No.2) Act 2005, Sch.10, para.10 and *supra*, para.38–18). As previously noted, it may be that the existence of such arrangements does not matter where an outgoing partner's share is transferred or accrues to the *continuing* partners and he is paid out the capital and current balances, etc., due to him, provided that this is outside the above three-year period. This would accord with the position which existed under the former stamp duty regime: see para.38–07. However, if this is correct, it would seem that, in such circumstances, the outgoing partner could also receive a payment by reference to a revaluation of the land owned by the firm without a charge to SDLT being incurred. This is more surprising, although the scope for a charge under the anti-avoidance provisions noted, *supra*, para.38–18 should not, in any event, be overlooked. What is clear is that if no money is withdrawn or other consideration in money or money's worth received, there will be no charge. This will seemingly include the case where sums due to an outgoing partner are transferred to a loan account.

Where SDLT is chargeable, this will be by reference to that proportion of the market value of the land owned by the partnership as is represented by the increase in each existing partner's income profit share (*ibid.* Sch.15, paras 14(6), (7)(b)) or, if an incoming partner acquired the outgoing partner's share, the proportion represented by that share (*ibid.* Sch.15, paras 14(6), (7)(a)), although special rules apply in the case of retirements within three years of an initial chargeable transfer to the firm (*ibid.* Sch.15, para.17A(7)).

Incoming partners

38–20   The admission of a partner is unlikely to involve a charge to SDLT unless he gives consideration for the acquisition of his share, *e.g.* by way of a premium. As previously noted (see *supra* para.38–17), the fact that he assumes liability for part of the firm's debts and obligations will seemingly not amount to consideration for this purpose, although the position may be otherwise where there is a partnership debt secured on the land. Where consideration *is* given, a proportion of the market value of the land owned by the partnership will be chargeable, as described *supra*, para.38–19. However, where there is a reduction of an existing partner's share in favour of an incoming partner within three years of the former transferring a chargeable interest to the firm, there will be a charge under *ibid.* Sch.15, para.17A (as added by the Finance (No.2) Act 2005, Sch.10, para.10) if the reduction is accompanied by a withdrawal of capital, etc. by that partner: see *supra*, para.38–18.

(4) *Dissolution of Partnership*

38–21   Where, on or following a dissolution, land owned by the partnership is trans-ferred *in specie* to a partner (or any person(s) to whom he is connected otherwise than as a partner), SDLT will be chargeable by reference to that proportion of the market value of the land as is equal to 100 minus "the sum of the lower proportions" (*i.e.* the same approach as described *supra*, para.38–16), although in this instance the comparison is as between the interest held by recipient partner and any connected partners after the transfer and their partnership shares imme-diately prior thereto: *ibid.* Sch.15, paras 18(1)–(3), (5), 20(1). It should be noted that special rules apply when determining the recipient partner's partnership share, according to whether the land was originally transferred to the firm before or after October 20, 2003 and, if the latter, whether stamp duty or SDLT was paid on the original transfer into the partnership: *ibid.* Sch.15, paras 21, 22. In certain circumstances, the recipient's share under these rules may be zero. Where actual consideration is given, such part as is equal to "the sum of the lower proportions" expressed as a percentage will also be chargeable: *ibid.* Sch.15, para.18(4). Where the consideration consists of or includes rent, different rules apply: *ibid.* Sch.15, paras 18(6), 19. It should be noted that this regime will also apply in the case of a distribution of a chargeable interest in land which is *deemed* to be partnership property by reason of its use for partnership purposes: *ibid.* Sch.15, para.34(1); see also *supra*, para.38–15.

A transfer of a chargeable interest will be regarded as taking place on or following a dissolution where land belonging to the partnership ceases to be partnership property or where a new chargeable interest is granted or created out of such land: *ibid.* Sch.15, para.37. Land held by a firm on its dissolution retains its character as partnership property until such time as a distribution occurs, irrespective of what the partners may have agreed and, seemingly, without limit of time: *ibid.* Sch.15, para.18(7).

If partners agree to retain land owned by the firm in the same proportions as their income profit shares immediately prior to the dissolution, it might be expected that no charge to SDLT would be imposed, but this is by no means clear since the legislation must seemingly be applied to each partner individually: see *ibid.* Sch.15, para.18(1)(a). It is difficult to see how the imposition of a charge in such circumstances could logically be justified, even where the special rules described above produce a deemed partnership share of zero. Equally, it must be recognised that, if no charge were imposed on the distribution, the land would cease to retain the character of partnership property (see *ibid.* Sch.15, para.37(a)) and would thereafter fall outwith partnership charging regime; *sed quaere.*

Special rules apply where the land is transferred out of a partnership which consists only of bodies corporate and "the sum of the lower proportions" is 75 or more (see *ibid.* Sch.15, para.24) and where the recipient of the transfer is another partnership and there is a potential chargeable transfer on the land being introduced into that other partnership (*ibid.* Sch.15, para.23).

Exemptions and reliefs

Schedule 15 of the Finance Act 2003 modifies the application of various forms **38–22** of relief in the context of certain of the partnership transactions described above: see *ibid.* paras 25 to 28.

APPENDICES

APPENDIX 1

PARTNERSHIP ACT 1890

Rules for determining existence of partnership (section 2)

As from a day to be appointed, the words ", widower, surviving civil partner" will be **A1–03** added after "widow" in subs.(3)(c) by the Civil Partnership Act 2004, Sch.27, para.2.

LIMITED PARTNERSHIPS ACT 1907

Definition and constitution of limited partnership (section 4)

A3–04   The words "shall not consist of more than twenty persons, and" in subs.(2) were, with effect from December 21, 2002, repealed by the Regulatory Reform (Reform of 20 Member Limit in Partnerships etc.) Order 2002 (SI 2002/3203), reg.3.

APPENDIX 6

HM REVENUE & CUSTOMS STATEMENTS OF PRACTICE AND OTHER MATERIALS

II. Capital Gains Tax

STATEMENT OF PRACTICE D12

PARTNERSHIPS

(Originally issued January 17, 1975, reissued on October 8, 2002 and updated to August 2003)

[NOTE: This Statement of Practice is, for convenience, reproduced in its entirety even though many of its provisions remain unchanged. The principle amendments are to the introduction and paras 1 and 12.]

This statement of practice was originally issued by the Board of Inland Revenue on 17 January 1975 following discussions with the Law Society and the Allied Accountancy Bodies on the Capital Gains Tax treatment of partnerships. This statement sets out a number of points of general practice which have been agreed in respect of partnerships to which TCGA 1992, s.59[1] applies. **A6–04**

The enactment of the Limited Liability Partnership Act 2000, has created, from April 2001, the concept of limited liability partnerships (as bodies corporate) in UK law. In conjunction with this, new Capital Gains Tax provisions dealing with such partnerships have been introduced through TCGA 1992, s.59A. TCGA 1992, s.59A(1) mirrors TCGA 1992, s.59[1] in treating any dealings in chargeable assets by a limited liability partnership as dealings by the individual members, as partners, for Capital Gains Tax purposes. Each member of a limited liability partnership to which s.59A(1) applies has therefore to be regarded, like a partner in any other (non-corporate) partnership, as owning a fractional share of each of the partnership assets and not an interest in the partnership itself.

This statement of practice has therefore been extended to limited liability partnerships which meet the requirements of TCGA 1992, s.59A(1), such that capital gains of a partnership fall to be charged on its members as partners. Accordingly, in the text of the statement of practice, all references to a 'partnership' or 'firm' include reference to limited liability partnerships to which TCGA 1992, s.59A(1) applies, and all references to

---

[1] See now the Taxation of Chargeable Gains Act 1992, s.59(1) (as renumbered): see *supra*, para.35–01.

'partner' include reference to a member of a limited liability partnership to which TCGA 1992, s.59A(1) applies.

For the avoidance of doubt, this statement of practice does not apply to the members of a limited liability partnership which ceases to be 'fiscally transparent' by reason of its not being, or its no longer being, within TCGA 1992, s.59A(1).

1. Valuation of a partner's share in a partnership asset

A6–05 Where it is necessary to ascertain the market value of a partner's share in a partnership asset for Capital Gains Tax purposes, it will be taken as a fraction of the value of the total partnership interest in the asset without any discount for the size of his share. If, for example, a partnership owned all the issued shares in a company, the value of the interest in that holding of a partner with a one-tenth share would be one-tenth of the value of the partnership's 100 per cent holding.

2. Disposals of assets by a partnership

A6–06 Where an asset is disposed of by a partnership to an outside party each of the partners will be treated as disposing of his fractional share of the asset. In computing gains or losses the proceeds of disposal will be allocated between the partners in the ratio of their share in asset surpluses at the time of disposal. Where this is not specifically laid down the allocation will follow the actual destination of the surplus as shown in the partnership accounts; regard will of course have to be paid to any agreement outside the accounts. If the surplus is not allocated among the partners but, for example, put to a common reserve, regard will be had to the ordinary profit sharing ratio in the absence of a specified asset-surplus-sharing ratio. Expenditure on the acquisition of assets by a partnership will be allocated between the partners in the same way at the time of the acquisition. This allocation may require adjustment, however, if there is a subsequent change in the partnership sharing ratios (see paragraph 4).

3. Partnership assets divided in kind among the partners

A6–07 Where a partnership distributes an asset in kind to one or more of the partners, for example on dissolution, a partner who receives the asset will not be regarded as disposing of his fractional share in it. A computation will first be necessary of the gains which would be chargeable on the individual partners if the asset has been disposed of at its current market value. Where this results in a gain being attributed to a partner not receiving the asset the gain will be charged at the time of the distribution of the asset. Where, however, the gain is allocated to a partner receiving the asset concerned there will be no charge on distribution. Instead, his Capital Gains Tax cost to be carried forward will be the market value of the asset at the date of distribution as reduced by the amount of his gain. The same principles will be applied where the computation results in a loss.

4. Changes in partnership sharing ratios

A6–08 An occasion of charge also arises when there is a change in partnership sharing ratios including changes arising from a partner joining or leaving the partnership. In these circumstances a partner who reduces or gives up his share in asset surpluses will be treated as disposing of part of the whole of his share in each of the partnership assets and a partner who increases his share will be treated as making a similar acquisition. Subject to the qualifications mentioned at 6 and 7 below the disposal consideration will be a fraction (equal to the fractional share changing hands) of the current balance sheet value of each chargeable asset provided there is no direct payment of consideration outside the partnership. Where no adjustment is made through the partnership accounts (for example, by revaluation of the assets coupled with a corresponding increase or decrease in the partner's current or capital account at some date between the partner's acquisition and the reduction in his share) the disposal is treated as made for a consideration equal to his Capital Gains Tax cost and thus there will be neither a chargeable gain nor an allowable loss at that point. A partner whose share reduces will carry forward a smaller proportion of cost to set against a subsequent disposal of the asset and a partner whose share increases will carry forward a larger proportion of cost.

The general rules in TCGA 1992, s.42 for apportioning the total acquisition cost on a part-disposal of an asset will not be applied in the case of a partner reducing his asset-surplus share. Instead, the cost of the part disposed of will be calculated on a fractional basis.

5. *Adjustment through the accounts*

Where a partnership asset is revalued a partner will be credited in his current or capital account with a sum equal to his fractional share of the increase in value. An upward revaluation of chargeable assets is not itself an occasion of charge. If, however, there were to be a subsequent reduction in the partner's asset-surplus share, the effect would be to reduce his potential liability to Capital Gains Tax on the eventual disposal of the assets without an equivalent reduction of the credit he has received in the accounts. Consequently at the time of the reduction in sharing ratio he will be regarded as disposing of the fractional share of the partnership asset represented by the difference between his old and his new share for a consideration equal to that fraction of the increased value at the revaluation. The partner whose share correspondingly increases will have his acquisition cost to be carried forward for the asset increased by the same amount. The same principles will be applied in the case of a downward revaluation.   **A6–09**

6. *Payments outside the accounts*

Where on a change of partnership sharing ratios payments are made directly between two or more partners outside the framework of the partnership accounts, the payments represent consideration for the disposal of the whole or part of a partner's share in partnership assets in addition to any consideration calculated on the basis described in 4 and 5 above. Often such payments will be for goodwill not included in the balance sheet. In such cases the partner receiving the payment will have no Capital Gains Tax cost to set against it unless he made a similar payment for his share in the asset (for example, on entering the partnership) or elects to have the market value at 6 April 1965 treated as his acquisition cost. The partner making the payment will only be allowed to deduct the amount in computing gains or losses on a subsequent disposal of his share in the asset. He will be able to claim a loss when he finally leaves the partnership or when his share is reduced provided that he then receives either no consideration or a lesser consideration for his share of the asset. Where the payment clearly constitutes payment for a share in assets included in the partnership accounts, the partner receiving it will be able to deduct the amount of the partnership acquisition cost represented by the fraction he is disposing of. Special treatment, as outlined in 7 below, may be necessary for transfers between persons not at arm's length.   **A6–10**

7. *Transfers between persons not at arm's length*

Where no payment is made either through or outside the accounts in connection with a change in partnership sharing ratio, a Capital Gains Tax charge will only arise if the transaction is otherwise than by way of a bargain made at arm's length and falls therefore within TCGA 1992, s.17 extended by TCGA 1992 s.18 for transactions between connected persons. Under TCGA 1992, s.286(4) transfers of partnership assets between partners are not regarded as transactions between connected persons if they are pursuant to genuine commercial arrangements. This treatment will also be given to transactions between an incoming partner and the existing partners.   **A6–11**

Where the partners (including incoming partners) are connected other than by partnership (for example, father and son) or are otherwise not at arm's length (for example, uncle and nephew) the transfer of a share in the partnership assets may fall to be treated as having been made at market value. Market value will not be substituted, however, if nothing would have been paid had the parties been at arm's length. Similarly if consideration of less than market value passes between partners connected other than by partnership or otherwise not at arm's length, the transfer will only be regarded as having been made for full market value if the consideration actually paid was less than that which would have been paid by parties at arm's length. Where a transfer has to be treated as if it had taken place for market value, the deemed disposal will fall to be treated in the same way as payments outside the accounts.

8. Annuities provided by partnerships

A6–12 A lump sum which is paid to a partner on leaving the partnership or on a reduction of his share in the partnership represents consideration for the disposal by the partner concerned of the whole or part of his share in the partnership assets and will be subject to the rules in 6 above. The same treatment will apply when a partnership buys a purchased life annuity for a partner, the measure of the consideration being the actual costs of the annuity.

Where a partnership makes annual payments to a retired partner (whether under covenant or not) the capitalised value of the annuity will only be treated as consideration for the disposal of his share in the partnership assets under TCGA 1992, s.37(3), if it is more than can be regarded as a reasonable recognition of the past contribution of work and effort by the partner to the partnership. Provided that the former partner had been in the partnership for at least ten years an annuity will be regarded as reasonable for this purpose if it is no more than two-thirds of his average share of the profits in the best three of the last seven years in which he was required to devote substantially the whole of this time to acting as a partner. In arriving at a partner's share of the profits regard will be had to the partnership profits assessed before deduction of any capital allowances or charges. The ten year period will include any period during which the partner was a member of another firm whose business has been merged with that of the present firm. For lesser periods the following fractions will be used instead of two-thirds:

Complete years in partnership	Fraction
1–5	1/60 for each year
6	8/60
7	16/60
8	24/60
9	32/60

Where the capitalised value of an annuity is treated as consideration received by the retired partner, it will also be regarded as allowable expenditure by the remaining partners on the acquisition of their fractional shares in partnership assets from him.

9. Mergers

A6–13 Where the members of two or more existing partnerships come together to form a new one, the Capital Gains Tax treatment will follow the same lines as that for changes in partnership sharing ratios. If gains arise for reasons similar to those covered in 5 and 6 above, it may be possible for rollover relief under TCGA 1992, s.152 to be claimed by any partner continuing in the partnership insofar as he disposes of part of his share in the assets of the old firm and acquires a share in other assets put into the 'merged' firm. Where, however, in such cases the consideration given for the shares in chargeable assets acquired is less than the consideration for those disposed of, relief will be restricted under TCGA 1992, s.153.

10. *Shares acquired in stages*

Where a share in a partnership is acquired in stages wholly after 5 April 1965, the **A6–14** acquisition costs of the various chargeable assets will be calculated by pooling the expenditure relating to each asset. Where a share built up in stages was acquired wholly or partly before 6 April 1965 the rules in TCGA 1992, Schedule 2, Para.18, will normally be followed to identify the acquisition cost of the share in each asset which is disposed of on the occasion of a reduction in the partnership's share; that is, the disposal will normally be identified with shares acquired on a 'first in, first out' basis. Special consideration will be given, however, to any case in which this rule appears to produce an unreasonable result when applied to temporary changes in the shares in a partnership, for example those occurring when a partner's departure and a new partner's arrival are out of step by a few months.

11. *Elections under TCGA 1992, Schedule 2, Para.4*

Where the assets disposed of are quoted securities eligible for a pooling election under **A6–15** paragraph 4 of TCGA 1992, Schedule 2, partners will be allowed to make separate elections in respect of shares or fixed interest securities held by the partnership as distinct from shares and securities which they hold on a personal basis. Each partner will have a separate right of election for his proportion of the partnership securities and the time limit for the purposes of Schedule 2 will run from the earlier of—

(a) the first relevant disposal of shares or securities by the partnership; and

(b) the first reduction of the particular partner's share in the partnership assets after 19 March 1968.

12. *Partnership goodwill and taper relief*

This paragraph applies where the value of goodwill which a partnership generates in the **A6–16** conduct of its business is not recognised in its balance sheet and where, as a matter of consistent practice, no value is placed on that goodwill in dealings between the partners. In such circumstances, the partnership goodwill will not be regarded as a 'fungible asset' (and, therefore, will not be within the definition of 'securities' in section TCGA 1992, s.104(3) for the purpose of Capital Gains Tax taper relief under TCGA 1992, s.2A). Accordingly, on a disposal for actual consideration of any particular partner's interest in the goodwill of such a partnership, that interest will be treated as the same asset (or, in the case of a part disposal, a part of the same asset) as was originally acquired by that partner when first becoming entitled to a share in the goodwill of that partnership.

The treatment described in the preceding paragraph will also be applied to goodwill acquired for consideration by a partnership but which is not, at any time, recognised in the partnership balance sheet at a value exceeding its cost of acquisition nor otherwise taken into account in dealings between partners. However, such purchased goodwill will continue to be treated for the purpose of computing capital gains tax taper relief as assets separate from the partnership's self-generated goodwill. On a disposal or part disposal for actual consideration of an interest in such purchased goodwill by any particular partner, that interest shall be treated for taper relief purposes as acquired either on the date of purchase by the partnership or on the date on which the disposing partner first became entitled to a share in that goodwill, whichever is the later.

IV. Value Added Tax

BUSINESS BRIEF 21/04 (AUGUST 10, 2004)

1. VAT: VAT position of share issues and partnership contributions following the European Court of Justice decision in *Kaphag Renditefonds*

A6–23   This Business Brief clarifies Customs' position on two issues arising from the decision of the European Court of Justice in the German case of *KapHag Renditefonds v. Finanzamt Charlottenburg* (Case C-442/01):

A—Whether the issue of shares constitutes a supply for VAT purposes; and

B—The VAT position of contributions to partnerships.

The case of *KapHag* concerned the admission of a new partner into a partnership on payment of a capital contribution. The European Court held that no supply was being made by either the individual partners or the partnership to the incoming partner in return for the capital contribution.

A—Whether the issue of shares constitutes a supply

A6–24   The *KapHag* decision has been cited as authority for the view that an issue of shares by a company is similarly not a supply for VAT purposes. It is claimed that an issue of shares therefore falls outside the terms of Item 6 of Group 5 of Schedule 9 to the Value Added Tax Act 1994. That Item exempts from VAT:

"The issue, transfer or receipt of, or any dealing with, any security or secondary security . . . "

It is Customs' view that the formation or variation of a partnership arrangement is wholly distinguishable from the position where a company issues shares in return for consideration. *KapHag* was concerned solely with the issues surrounding a partnership. The VAT treatment of share issues has been considered by the Court of Appeal in *Trinity Mirror plc* ([2001] S.T.C. 192) where it was held that an issue of shares by a company did constitute a supply of services for VAT purposes and these fall to be exempt under Item 6 of Group 5 of Schedule 9 to the Act. In most circumstances there will then be a restriction of input tax under the partial exemption rules. Further information is available from VAT Notice 706 Partial Exemption.

B—Contributions to partnerships

A6–25   Partnerships to which this section applies include "normal" partnerships of individuals or corporate bodies, limited partnerships whose members are individuals or corporate bodies, overseas limited partnerships that are registered as "normal" partnerships or corporate bodies and limited liability partnerships.

Background

In *KapHag*, the incoming partner was contributing cash in return for admission into the partnership but it will often be the case that the contribution is in the form of other assets. For example, a new partner's contribution may comprise land or interests in land. The European Court's decision tacitly accepted the Advocate-General's Opinion that the same principles would apply whether the contribution consisted of cash or other assets. Whatever the nature of the assets comprising the contribution, there is no reciprocal supply from the partnership. However, where the assets are not cash, the making of the partnership contribution may have other VAT consequences.

The Advocate-General was satisfied that there was "no doubt that the new partner is effecting an act of disposal of his assets, for which the admission to the partnership is not the consideration" (Paragraph 33 of the Opinion). Such a disposal can therefore have VAT consequences when the partner contributing the assets is a VAT registered person. These consequences will vary depending on the nature of the assets being contributed.

KapHag establishes that nothing is provided by the partnership in return for the assets contributed, therefore any such disposal by the incoming partner is made for no consideration. The VAT Act provides that certain things are subject to VAT even when they are provided or done for no consideration. Customs' view is that all those provisions will still apply where there is no consideration when there is a contribution to partnership assets. A VAT registered person may therefore have to account for tax if he contributes assets to the partnership in the circumstances described in the Act. The VAT consequences can be considered under several main heads:

   (i) Contribution to partnership comprising services;

  (ii) Contribution to partnership comprising goods other than land;

 (iii) Contribution to partnership comprising land or interests in land;

 (iv) Whether contribution to partnership can constitute the transfer of a going concern;

  (v) How the partnership can reclaim the output tax accounted for by an incoming partner on his contribution as its input tax;

 (vi) Capital Goods Scheme consequences; and

(vii) Transfer of assets out of a partnership.

(i) *Contribution to partnership comprising services*

A partnership contribution may comprise services rather than goods—examples of this   **A6–26** could be a trademark or trading logo or the use of an asset the ownership of which is retained by the incoming partner. Two legislative provisions set out the circumstances in which such a contribution may be regarded as a taxable supply, paragraph 5(4) of Schedule 4 to the VAT Act and the Value Added Tax (Supply of Services) Order 1993 (SI 1993/1507).

A supply can arise under paragraph 5(4) where a taxable person applies business goods to private use or makes them available for purposes other than those of his business. The taxable person or his predecessor must have been entitled to input tax under sections 25 and 26 of the VAT Act on the supply of those goods (or anything comprised in them) to him.

The Supply of Services Order similarly provides that a supply arises where a taxable person applies bought-in services to private or non-business use for no consideration where he has been entitled to input tax credit under sections 25 and 26. The value of such a supply cannot exceed the taxable person's input tax entitlement.

Where the above criteria are satisfied, a VAT registered incoming partner will have to account for tax on the supply of services that he is regarded as making in the disposal of the services from his existing business. The partnership may be able to recover this as its input tax where the contributed services are to be used for its business. The procedure for doing this is described at (v) below.

(ii) Contribution to partnership comprising goods other than land

A6–27 If a partnership contribution comprises goods other than land that a taxable person (the transferor) held as assets, then a deemed supply will be generated as a result of Paragraph 5(1) of Schedule 4 to the VAT Act. This deemed supply does not require there to be consideration when the goods are transferred. It does however only apply where the taxable person disposing of the goods, or their predecessor, if for example they obtained the goods by way of a TOGC, was entitled to full or partial credit for the VAT charged when the goods were supplied to him. Where such a deemed supply arises, the incoming partner will have to account for VAT. The partnership may be able to recover this as its input tax where the contributed assets are to be used for its business. The procedure for doing this is described at (v) below.

(iii) Contribution to partnership comprising land or interests in land

A6–28 The VAT treatment of land or interests in land also depends upon whether the incoming partner or his predecessor was entitled to deduct input tax in relation to the property that he is contributing to the partnership. For example, if he had opted to tax the property, or it was inherently taxable like new freehold commercial property, there may be a deemed supply as described at (ii) above. The incoming partner will then have to account for VAT on this supply. As with other contributed goods, the partnership may be entitled to recover this as input tax where the property is to be used for the partnership's business. The procedure for doing this is described at (v) below.

Please note all submitted notifications of an option to tax need to be signed by "an authorised signatory" as described in paragraph 7.1 of VAT Notice 742A Opting to tax Land & Buildings.

(iv) Whether contribution to partnership can constitute the transfer of a going concern

A6–29 It is possible that when assets are transferred by way of a partnership contribution that this could qualify to be treated as a transfer of a going concern (Section 49 of the VAT Act and Article 5 of the VAT (Special Provisions) Order 1995 (SI 1995/1268)). If the contribution meets the conditions to be treated as a transfer of a going concern no VAT will be due from the transferor.

(v) How the partnership can reclaim the output tax accounted for by an incoming partner on his contribution as its input tax

A6–30 When an incoming partner contributes goods and/or services (on which VAT is due as described above) and the partnership uses them for its business purposes, the partnership can recover the VAT as input tax subject to the normal rules. The incoming partner cannot issue a tax invoice, but in order to provide the partnership with acceptable evidence to support a claim for recovery of input tax, he may use his normal invoicing documentation overwritten with the following statement:

> "*Certificate for Tax on Partnership Contribution*
> No payment is necessary for these goods/services. Output tax has been accounted for on the supply."

The incoming partner must show full details of the goods and/or services on the documentation and the amount of VAT shown must be the amount of output tax accounted for to Customs and Excise.

(vi) Capital Goods Scheme consequences

A6–31 Where the capital contribution is in the form of an interest in land or a computer, it may be an existing capital item of the incoming partner under the Capital Goods Scheme

(CGS). If the transfer to the partnership constitutes a supply which is a disposal of an existing CGS item, then this will wind up the existing CGS item and a disposal adjustment may be due. If the transfer constitutes a TOGC then this will end the current interval for the incoming partner and the partnership will then be responsible for making adjustments for any remaining intervals.

As transfers of assets capital contributions will always constitute either a supply or a TOGC, any existing CGS items will always either be subject to a disposal adjustment or continuing CGS adjustments.

Even if the asset transferred as a capital contribution is not a CGS item in the hands of the incoming partner, it may create a new CGS item for the partnership when its transfer constitutes a supply. If this happens the partnership will need to make adjustments in subsequent intervals in the normal way.

The CGS is further explained in VAT Notice 706/2 Capital Goods Scheme.

(vii) *Transfer of assets out of a partnership*

KapHag was only concerned with assets moving into a partnership in the form of a   **A6–32** partnership contribution. It did not cover the reverse situation, where partnership assets are paid out to an outgoing partner or otherwise disposed of by the partnership for no consideration. Where a transfer of assets out of a partnership for no consideration occurs, one of the following sets of circumstances will apply.

(a) If the incoming partner accounted for output tax when he contributed the assets to the partnership and the partnership was entitled to recover all or part of this as its input tax, there will be a subsequent supply by the partnership when the same assets are transferred out unless the transfer out now satisfies the TOGC criteria.

(b) If no output tax was accounted for when the assets were contributed to the partnership because they constituted a TOGC, the transfer out of the same assets will be a deemed supply upon which the partnership will have to account for tax unless the TOGC criteria are again satisfied.

(c) The partnership may be transferring out more assets than those originally contributed to it. Although the original contribution to the partnership may not have been a TOGC, the subsequent transfer out may now satisfy the TOGC criteria. If it does, no VAT will be due from the partnership.

(d) The original contribution to the partnership may have been a TOGC but the partnership may now be transferring out less of the assets than were originally contributed. Unless the assets being transferred out still meet the TOGC criteria in their own right, there may be a deemed supply upon which the partnership will have to account for the appropriate tax. As explained at (ii) and (iii) above, the entitlement of the partnership or its predecessor to deduct input tax in relation to the items that are the subject of the transfer out will determine whether or not there is a supply.

Application of section 45 of the VAT Act 1994

In the past, there was uncertainty as to whether it was section 45(1) of the VAT Act that   **A6–33** led to there being no supply from a partnership to an incoming partner. That section provides for the registration of partnerships in the following terms:

"45(1) The registration under this Act of persons—

(a) carrying on a business in partnership, or

(b) carrying on in partnership any other activities in the course or furtherance of which they acquire goods from other member States, may be in the name of the firm; and no account shall be taken, in determining for any purpose of this Act whether goods or services are supplied to or by such persons or are acquired by such persons from another member State, of any change in the partnership."

Partnerships in England and Wales have no legal identity. A new partner joining a partnership, or old one leaving it, would result in a new partnership rather than change the composition of the existing one. Without s.45(1), deregistration and registration would be necessary every time a partner joined or left. The purpose of s.45(1) is to ensure continuity by providing that a business carried on in a firm's name is treated as a continuing business irrespective of changes in its composition. The situation addressed by s.45(1) is therefore entirely different to that considered in *KapHag*.

Further information

Further information on this change is available from Customs' National Advice Service on 0845 010 9000. This number should also be used for general enquiries.

[The remainder of this Business Brief is not reproduced.]

BUSINESS BRIEF 30/04 (NOVEMBER 19, 2004)

VAT AND PARTNERSHIP "SHARES"

Background

A6–34 Business Brief 21/04 clarified Customs' policy on share issues and partnership contributions following the European Court of Justice (ECJ) decision in *KapHag Renditefonds* (C-442/01). That Business Brief did not deal with the VAT position of transfers of partnership interests ("shares"). This Business Brief explains the VAT treatment of transactions involving the transfer of a partner's "share".

Is the disposal of a "share" in a partnership a supply?

KapHag established that a partnership entity or the existing partners are making no supply when a new partner is admitted in return for making a capital contribution. The question arises whether the subsequent disposal by the partner of that "share" in the partnership is a supply for VAT purposes. It is important to bear in mind that this "share" is distinct from the assets that were contributed by the partner when they joined the partnership. Therefore, even though the selling price of the "share" may be determined by the value of those assets, they are not the subject of the later sale, which has its own liability for VAT purposes.

Although the ECJ has not considered this type of transaction with respect to partnership "shares", there have been a number of cases where it has given a decision in respect of transactions involving shares in companies. The cases of *Polysar* (C-60/90), *Harnas and Helm* (C-C-80/95), *Wellcome Trust* (C-155/94) and *Regie Dauphinoise* (C-306/94) have established that the mere acquisition and holding of shares in a company is not to be regarded as an economic activity. However, it has stated that transactions in shares or interests in companies and associations may constitute economic activity in three situations:

    (a) Where the transactions constitute the direct, permanent and necessary extension of an economic activity.

(b) Where the transactions are effected in order to secure a direct or indirect involvement in the management of a company in which the holding is acquired.

(c) Where the transactions are effected as part of a commercial share-dealing activity.

Customs considers that the same principles apply to transactions involving partnership "shares". This means that in some circumstances the disposal of a partnership "share" will not constitute a supply and in others it will.

Circumstances in which the disposal of a partnership "share" will not constitute a supply

This list is not exhaustive. The most common situations in which the disposal of a partnership "share" by a partner will not be a supply are likely to be: **A6–35**

1. *The "share" is disposed of for no consideration*—A "share" in a partnership comprises services rather than goods. When services are transferred, assigned or otherwise disposed of for no consideration, they do not constitute any supply for VAT purposes.

2. *The "share" being sold was acquired simply as an investment*—Where a partner has acquired his "share" merely to secure a share in any future profits and has had no involvement in running the partnership, the subsequent sale or assignment of that "share" for consideration will not be an economic activity. This will not constitute any supply for VAT purposes.

Circumstances in which the disposal of a partnership "share" will constitute a supply

Again, this list is not exhaustive. The most common situations in which the disposal of a partnership "share" by a partner will be a supply are likely to be: **A6–36**

1. *Where the partnership "share" was acquired and disposed of as a direct extension of the partner's economic activities*—Where a partner is a taxable person in their own right, the partnership "share" may have been acquired in the course or furtherance of their own economic activities. If that is the case, the subsequent transfer or assignment of that "share" for a consideration will also be economic activity of that taxable person. For example, the partner may have a business asset to be sold and, rather than selling the asset directly, may have contributed that asset into a partnership and sold the resultant partnership "share" instead. The sale of that partnership "share" will constitute a supply for VAT purposes.

2. *Where the partnership "share" was acquired in order to obtain an active role in the business of the partnership*—Where a partner is a taxable person in their own right and had acquired the partnership "share" in order to actively participate in, or control, the business of the partnership, then the sale of that "share" can be economic activity on the partner's part. The sale of the "share" will constitute a supply for VAT purposes.

3. *Where the partnership "share" was acquired as part of a commercial partnership "share-dealing" activity*—A partner who is a taxable person may have a business of dealing in partnership "shares". This will be economic activity on the partner's part. Sales or assignments of the partnership "shares" that were acquired in the course of this activity that are for a consideration will constitute supplies for VAT purposes.

For the avoidance of any doubt, you should note that supplies of partnership "shares" in the above circumstances cannot be disregarded by virtue of section 45(1) of the VAT

Act 1994. As Business Brief 21/04 explained, the purpose of s.45 (1) is to ensure continuity by providing that changes in the composition of a partnership do not create the need for a partnership to deregister and re-register for VAT every time the partners change. It also makes it unnecessary to take account of any changes in the composition of the partnership when determining what supplies have been made or received by the partnership business. The section has no effect upon any supply that one of the partners may be making as a taxable person in their own right.

Liability of supplies of partnership shares

A6–37 In those circumstances where the disposal of a partnership "share" is a supply, that supply will be an exempt financial service.

Treatment of VAT on associated purchases

A6–38 Where the disposal of an existing partnership "share" is not a supply, the VAT incurred in connection with the disposal will normally not be input tax. Where the disposal is a supply, the related VAT will be input tax, but recovery will normally be fully restricted under the partial exemption rules as the supply is exempt. This is subject to the de minimis provisions (see VAT Notice 706 'Partial Exemption').

Application to past transactions

A6–39 This Business Brief clarifies existing policy and the above principles will be applied to all future transactions. Where a past transaction has been treated differently from the above and resulted in an underdeclaration Customs will take no further action. If a past transaction has been treated differently and resulted in an overdeclaration, businesses may use the voluntary disclosure procedure to reclaim the VAT. Any such claims will be subject to the "three-year capping rules" and rules relating to the payment of statutory interest.

Further information

For further help and advice please contact Customs' National Advice Service on 0845 010 9000.

Source: HM Revenue & Customs
© Crown Copyright

INDEX

[References preceded by the letter A are to the statutory and other materials contained in the Appendices.]